14 Days Prayer

of

Deliverance

From

Witchcraft Attacks

TIMOTHY ATUNNISE

TSA SOLUTION PUBLISHING
ATLANTA, GEORGIA

DELIVERANCE FROM WITCHCRAFT ATTACKS

Unless otherwise specified, all Scripture quotations in this book are from The Holy Bible, King James Version. KJV is Public domain in the United States printed in 1987.

GLOVIM PUBLICATIONS
1078 Citizens Pkwy
Suite A
Morrow, Georgia 30260
glovimbooks@gmail.com
www.glovimonline.org

TSA Solution Publishing
A division of Timat Store, LLC.
Atlanta, GA 30294
timatstore@yahoo.com

Cover Design: Tim Atunnise

Printed in the United States of America

IMPORTANT NOTICE

Deliverance is a benefit of the Kingdom, only for the children of God. If you have not accepted Jesus Christ as your personal Lord and Savior, this is the best time to do so.

Before you continue, you need to be sure you are in the right standing with God if you want to exercise authority and power in the name of Jesus Christ. The Bible says,
"Then he called his twelve disciples together, and gave them power and authority over all devils, and to cure diseases." - Luke 9:1

"And these signs shall follow them that believe; in my name shall they cast out devils; they shall speak with new tongues; they shall take up serpents; and if they drink any deadly thing, it shall not hurt them; they shall lay hands on the sick, and they shall recover." – Mark 16:17-18.

These are promises for the Children of God, not just for everyone. Why don't you give your life to Christ today and you will have access to the same promises. Food that is meant for the children will not be given to the dogs.

"But he answered and said, it is not meet to take the children's bread, and cast it to dogs" – Matthew 15:26.

If you really want to be delivered from any bondage of the wicked and be set free from any form of captivity, I ask you today to give your life to Christ. If you are ready, say this prayer with all your heart:

"Dear Heavenly Father, You have called me to Yourself in the name of Your dear Son Jesus Christ. I realize that Jesus Christ is the only Way, the Truth, and the Life.

I acknowledge to You that I am a sinner. I believe that Your only begotten Son Jesus Christ shed His precious blood on the cross, died for my sins, and rose again on the third day. I am truly sorry for the deeds which I have committed against You, and therefore, I am willing to repent (turn away from my sins). Have mercy on me, a sinner. Cleanse me, and forgive me of my sins.

I truly desire to serve You, Lord Jesus. Starting from now, I pray that You would help me to hear Your still small voice. Lord, I desire to be led by Your Holy Spirit so I can faithfully follow You and obey all of Your commandments. I ask You for the strength to love You more than anything else so I won't fall back into my old ways. I also ask You to bring genuine believers into my life who will encourage me to live for You and help me stay accountable.

Jesus, I am truly grateful for Your grace which has led me to repentance and has saved me from my sins. By the indwelling of Your Holy Spirit, I now have the power to overcome all sin which before so easily entangled me. Lord Jesus, please transform my life so that I may bring glory and honor to You alone and not to myself.

Right now I confess Jesus Christ as the Lord of my life. With my heart, I believe that God the Father raised His Son Jesus Christ from the dead. This very moment I acknowledge that Jesus Christ is my Savior and according to His Word, right now I am born again. Thank You Jesus, for coming into my life and hearing my prayer. I ask all of this in the name of my Lord and Savior, Jesus Christ. Amen".

I hereby congratulate and welcome you into the Kingdom. You hereby have full access to the benefits, promises and blessings of the Kingdom.

This book is loaded with blessings, you will not be disappointed as you continue to enjoy the goodness of the Lord.

INSTRUCTIONS

If you are new to this method of prayer, please follow this instruction carefully:

Step 1:

Spend enough time in praising and worshiping God not just for what He is about to do or what He has done, but WHO HE IS.

Step 2:

Unforgiveness will surely hinder your prayer, take time to remember all those who have done you wrong, and forgive them from the bottom of your heart. THIS IS VERY IMPORTANT BECAUSE YOUR DELIVERANCE DEPENDS ON IT.

Step 3:

Believe in your heart that God will answer your prayer when you call upon Him, and do not doubt in your heart.

Step 4:

Pray in the name of Jesus Christ alone.

Step 5:

Repeat each prayer point 25 to 30 times or until you are convinced that you receive answer before you go to the next prayer point. Example: When you take prayer point number 1, you say this prayer over and over again, 25 – 30 times or until you are convinced that you have an answer before you go to prayer point number 2.

Step 6:

It will be more effective if you can fast along with your prayer. If you want total deliverance from your bondage, take 3 days of sacrifice in fasting as you say your prayer aggressively, asking your situation to receive permanent solution and YOUR DELIVERANCE WILL BE MADE PERFECT IN THE NAME OF JESUS CHRIST. AMEN!

Table of Contents

Important Notice..4

Instructions..7

Day One...11

Day Two...23

Day Three...33

Day Four...43

Day Five...51

Day Six...61

Day Seven...69

Day Eight...77

Day Nine...89

Day Ten...97

Day Eleven..105

Day Twelve...119

Day Thirteen...129

Day Fourteen..137

But this kind does not go out except by prayer and fasting.
-    Matthew 17:21

DAY ONE

WAR AGAINST THE POWER OF WITCHCRAFT

Passages To Read Before You Pray:
Exodus 22:18, Isaiah 8:9-10, Ephesians 6:10-18,
Psalms 3, 35, 55, 109, 83

In the book of Job 22:28, the Scripture says when I decree a thing, it shall be established for me. I stand on this Scripture and decree. I have come into the presence of God today to plead my case. I enter through the gate of praise into the sanctuary of heaven. I cover myself in the precious blood of Jesus Christ. I baptize myself in the fire of the Holy Ghost. I charge this atmosphere with the fire of God, and I take this neighborhood for the Lord. I arrest every principality and power, territorial spirit, and every throne and kingdom that is not of God. I cast you down and I command you never to lift yourself up against me, because I have the life of God in me.

In the name of Jesus Christ, I confess my sins today, and I ask you O Lord to forgive me on the basis of your mercy. With all my heart, I forgive those who have sinned against me from the past through this moment. I release them from any form of guilt and shame, in the name of Jesus Christ. I hereby plead the blood of Jesus over any sins committed by my parents and ancestors. I cancel through the Blood of Jesus Christ, any satanic covenants, exchanges, vows or transactions made over my life, body, soul, spirit, and circumstances, in the name of Jesus Christ. I cancel every legal right that the devil may have against me, by the blood of Jesus Christ. The accuser of the brethren will have nothing against me as I come to the presence of God in prayer.

The devil cannot hinder or delay my prayer, because I know who I am. I am a child of the Kingdom; I am a king and priest of the Lord, redeemed from the hand of the devil by the blood of Jesus Christ. I declare that all satanic thrones, altars, dominions, principalities, powers, rulers of darkness, queen of the coast, queen of heavens, household wickedness, spiritual hosts of wickedness and all satanic works, have no power or authority over my life. I declare that satanic harassment and intimidation have no effect on me.

Today I receive divine strength to pray; I will not pray in vain. I will not pray amiss. My prayers will bring the desired results. I command the fountain of prayer to open now, and flow into my life, I command the warring angels of God to descend and fight on my behalf. Every minute and every hour that I spend in prayer will bring solution. Every prayer point will attract divine attention and divine intervention. I decree open heavens over my prayers, and today, God of heaven and earth will attend to my case. My prayers today will shake the heavens and move the earth; testimonies, miracles, healing, breakthrough, signs and wonders will follow my prayers. At the end of this prayer session, my life will never be the same again.

PRAYER POINTS

1. O God my Father, thank you for being my God, my Father and my friend.
2. O God my Father, thank you for the privilege to know you and the power of the resurrection of Jesus Christ.
3. O God my Father, thank you for always being there for me and with me.

4. O God my Father, thank you for the great and mighty things that you are doing in my life.

5. O God my Father, thank you for your provision and protection over me and my household.

6. O God my Father, thank you for always answering my prayers.

7. I confess my sins before you today and I ask you to forgive me on the basis of your mercy, in the name of Jesus Christ.

8. Wash me clean today O Lord by the blood of Jesus Christ.

9. I cover myself and my household with the blood of Jesus Christ.

10. My prayers today will not go in vain; my prayers will produce the desired results in the name of Jesus Christ.

11. By the power and authority in the name of Jesus Christ, I command every planting of the enemy in my life to be uprooted and destroyed, in the name of Jesus Christ.

12. By the power and authority in the name of Jesus Christ, I command every planting of the enemy in the life of my spouse to be uprooted and destroyed, in the name of Jesus Christ.

13. By the power and authority in the name of Jesus Christ, I command every planting of the enemy in the life of my children to be uprooted and destroyed, in the name of Jesus Christ.

14. By the power and authority in the name of Jesus Christ, I command every planting of the enemy in my finances to be uprooted and destroyed, in the name of Jesus Christ.

15. By the power and authority in the name of Jesus Christ, I command every planting of the enemy in my business to be uprooted and destroyed, in the name of Jesus Christ.

16. By the power and authority in the name of Jesus Christ, I command every planting of the enemy in my ministry to be uprooted and destroyed, in the name of Jesus Christ.

17. By the power and authority in the name of Jesus Christ, I command every planting of the enemy in my marriage to be uprooted and destroyed, in the name of Jesus Christ.

18. By the power in the blood of Jesus Christ, I arrest all satanic projections prepared against me and my household, in the name of Jesus Christ.

19. By the power in the blood of Jesus Christ, I command fiery darts of the enemy fired against me and my family to backfire, in the name of Jesus Christ.

20. By the power in the blood of Jesus Christ, I command satanic arrows fired against me and my family to backfire, in the name of Jesus Christ.

21. By the power in the blood of Jesus Christ, I cancel all witchcraft activities in any area of my life and I nullify all the effects, in the name of Jesus Christ.

22. By the power and authority in the name of Jesus Christ, I decree that the enemy is permanently denied access into my life, in the name of Jesus Christ.

23. By the power and authority in the name of Jesus Christ, I decree that the enemy is permanently denied access into my destiny, in the name of Jesus Christ.

24. By the power and authority in the name of Jesus Christ, I decree that the enemy is permanently denied access into my home, in the name of Jesus Christ.

25. By the power and authority in the name of Jesus Christ, I decree that the enemy is permanently denied access into my marriage, in the name of Jesus Christ.

26. By the power and authority in the name of Jesus Christ, I decree that the enemy is permanently denied access into my business, in the name of Jesus Christ.

27. By the power and authority in the name of Jesus Christ, I decree that the enemy is permanently denied access into my finances, in the name of Jesus Christ.

28. By the power and authority in the name of Jesus Christ, I decree that the enemy is permanently denied access into my family, in the name of Jesus Christ.

29. Today, I take and maintain my position; seated in Christ Jesus in heavenly places, and the devil is under my feet, in the name of Jesus Christ.

30. From this moment, I walk in dominion, power, and God's prophetic purpose, in the name of Jesus Christ.

31. By the power and authority in the name of Jesus Christ, I decree today that my purpose and destiny will be fulfilled now; without delay or interference, in the name of Jesus Christ.

32. By the power and authority in the name of Jesus Christ, I decree that divine timing shall manifest continually in my life, in the name of Jesus Christ.

33. By the power and authority in the name of Jesus Christ, I decree that divine connection shall manifest continually in my life, in the name of Jesus Christ.

34. By the power and authority in the name of Jesus Christ, I decree that strategic relationships shall manifest continually in my life, in the name of Jesus Christ.

35. By the power and authority in the name of Jesus Christ, I decree that open doors shall manifest continually in my life, in the name of Jesus Christ.

36. By the power and authority in the name of Jesus Christ, I decree that favor in high places shall manifest continually in my life, in the name of Jesus Christ.
37. I command divine solutions for every problem in my life to manifest now, in the name of Jesus Christ.
38. I command every satanic mystery concerning my life to be permanently exposed and decoded by the blood of Jesus Christ, in the name of Jesus Christ.
39. I command every evil cycle in my life to be permanently broken by the blood of Jesus Christ, in the name of Jesus Christ.
40. I command every satanic mechanism in any area of my life to be permanently destroyed by the fire of God, in the name of Jesus Christ.
41. I stand on the Word of God and I command every legality issued against me in the realms of the spirit to be overturned, in the name of Jesus Christ.
42. I stand on the Word of God and I command every technicality issued against me in the realms of the spirit to be overturned, in the name of Jesus Christ.
43. I stand on the Word of God and I command every judgment issued against me in the realms of the spirit to be overturned, in the name of Jesus Christ.
44. I stand on the Word of God and I command divine restraining order to be issued and enforced against all acts of injustices against me, in the name of Jesus Christ.
45. I stand on the Word of God and I command divine restraining order to be issued and enforced against satanic harassment in any area of my life, in the name of Jesus Christ.
46. I stand on the Word of God and I command divine restraining order to be issued and enforced against

household wickedness troubling my life, in the name of Jesus Christ.

47. I stand on the Word of God and I command divine restraining order to be issued and enforced against Jezebel's spirit manipulating me, in the name of Jesus Christ.

48. I stand on the Word of God and I command divine restraining order to be issued and enforced against satanic monitoring agents assigned against me, in the name of Jesus Christ.

49. I stand on the Word of God and I command divine restraining order to be issued and enforced against powers of darkness tormenting me day and night, in the name of Jesus Christ.

50. I stand on the Word of God and I command divine restraining order to be issued and enforced against my oppressors, in the name of Jesus Christ.

51. By the power in the name of Jesus Christ, I decree today that divine order for my restoration is signed with the blood of the Lamb, and enforced by the angels of God on every level, in the name of Jesus Christ.

52. I decree that my victory shall be announced and published throughout heaven, on earth and underneath the earth, in the name of Jesus Christ.

53. I decree today that all my shame and reproach shall be washed away by the blood of Jesus Christ, and I shall receive double honor, in the name of Jesus Christ.

54. O God my Father, let the blood of Jesus speak better things continually into my life, in the name of Jesus Christ.

55. O God my Father, let the blood of Jesus speak better things continually into my home, in the name of Jesus Christ.

56. O God my Father, let the blood of Jesus speak better things continually into my marriage, in the name of Jesus Christ.

57. O God my Father, let the blood of Jesus speak better things continually into my finances, in the name of Jesus Christ.

58. O God my Father, let the blood of Jesus speak better things continually into the life of my spouse, in the name of Jesus Christ.

59. O God my Father, let the blood of Jesus speak better things continually into the lives of my children, in the name of Jesus Christ.

60. O God my Father, let the blood of Jesus silence every accusation against me; whether it is true or false, in the name of Jesus Christ.

61. O God my Father, let the blood of Jesus locate, arrest and bind every power operating behind the scene against me and my family, in the name of Jesus Christ.

62. O God my Father, let the blood of Jesus locate, arrest and bind anybody anywhere accusing me day and night, in the name of Jesus Christ.

63. O God my Father, let the blood of Jesus locate, arrest and bind every tongue speaking evil against me, in the name of Jesus Christ.

64. By the power and authority in the name of Jesus Christ, I command every strongman operating in my life to be stripped of his authority over me and my family, in the name of Jesus Christ.

65. By the power and authority in the name of Jesus Christ, I command every strongman operating in my life to be stripped of his assignments concerning me and my family, in the name of Jesus Christ.

66. I bind every strongman and household wickedness working against me, and I destroy all their weapons by the fire of God, in the name of Jesus Christ.

67. I bind every strongman and household wickedness working against my spouse, and I destroy all their weapons by the fire of God, in the name of Jesus Christ.

68. I bind every strongman and household wickedness working against my children, and I destroy all their weapons by the fire of God, in the name of Jesus Christ.

69. I bind every strongman and household wickedness working against the plan of God for me, and I destroy all their weapons by the fire of God, in the name of Jesus Christ.

70. I bind every strongman and household wickedness working against my advancement, and I destroy all their weapons by the fire of God, in the name of Jesus Christ.

71. I bind every strongman and household wickedness working against my promotion, and I destroy all their weapons by the fire of God, in the name of Jesus Christ.

72. I bind every strongman and household wickedness working against my breakthroughs, and I destroy all their weapons by the fire of God, in the name of Jesus Christ.

73. I bind every strongman and household wickedness working against my success, and I destroy all their weapons by the fire of God, in the name of Jesus Christ.

74. I bind every strongman and household wickedness working against my marriage, and I destroy all their weapons by the fire of God, in the name of Jesus Christ.
75. I bind every strongman and household wickedness working against my finances, and I destroy all their weapons by the fire of God, in the name of Jesus Christ.
76. As a king and priest for God, I command the angels of heaven to capture the ground troops of the devil sent to attack me and my family, and put them in everlasting chains, in the name of Jesus Christ.
77. As a king and priest for God, I command the ground troops of the devil sent against me and my family to be stripped of their power, in the name of Jesus Christ.
78. As a king and priest for God, I command the ground troops of the devil sent against me and my family to be desensitized and permanently disorganized, in the name of Jesus Christ.
79. I overthrow the wisdom tables of the wicked and scatter them by the fire of God wherever and whenever they gather, in the name of Jesus Christ.
80. I release weapons of mass destruction upon the headquarters of my enemies and destroy all their weapons, in the name of Jesus Christ.
81. I release weapons of mass destruction upon the headquarters of my enemies and destroy all their means of retaliation, in the name of Jesus Christ.
82. By the power and authority in the name of Jesus Christ, today I possess the gates of my enemies, in the name of Jesus Christ.
83. By the power and authority in the name of Jesus Christ, I advance, take and rule the territory of my enemies, by

the power of the Holy Ghost, in the name of Jesus Christ.

84. I cover myself in the blood of Jesus Christ and repossess everything that the enemy has taken from me, in the name of Jesus Christ.

85. I claim victory today by the blood of the Lamb and the word of my testimony over every situation, circumstance, poverty, infirmity and every work of the devil, in the name of Jesus Christ.

I cover my prayers in the blood of Jesus Christ. According to the Word of God, I have asked, I shall receive. I have knocked the door, it shall be opened unto me. I have sought, I shall find, in the name of Jesus Christ. It is written, "… Decree a thing, and it shall be established". As I have spoken in prayer, it shall be so. My prayers shall produce desire results. My prayers shall produce desired miracles. My prayers shall produce desired testimonies, in the name of Jesus Christ. Territorial spirit and power cannot hinder this prayer. Sins and flesh cannot hinder this prayer. It is done. It is sealed by the blood of Jesus Christ. It is delivered to me, in Jesus might name. Amen!

DAY TWO

DELIVERANCE FROM WITCHCRAFT ATTACKS

Passages To Read Before You Pray:
Exodus 22:18, Galatians 3:13, Isaiah 49:24-26,
Isaiah 50:7-9, Psalms 3, 9, 35, 55, 69

In the book of Job 22:28, the Scripture says when I decree a thing, it shall be established for me. I stand on this Scripture and decree. I have come today to fellowship with my heavenly Father, and make my requests and needs known unto Him. I cannot be hindered nor delayed because I know who I am in the Lord. I am a child of the Kingdom, born of the Spirit, redeemed by the blood of Jesus Christ. I walk in authority, living life without any apology because the power and authority has been given to me according to the Word of God in the book of Luke 9:1.

As I have come to pray today and to fellowship with my heavenly Father, I cover myself in the blood of Jesus Christ, and I put on the whole armor of God. I hereby come against every Prince of Persia that wants to hinder my prayer, I arrest you by the power in the blood of Jesus Christ, I bind you and cast you down into the pit of hell.

I come against principalities and powers that wrestle with me and my prayers, I arrest you today by the power in the name of Jesus Christ, I bind you and cast you down into the pit of hell. I come against the rulers of the darkness of this world, against spiritual wickedness in high places, I arrest you all by the power in the name of Jesus Christ, I bind you and cast you down into the pit of hell. I come against weakness and weariness, I arrest you today by the power in the name of Jesus Christ, I bind you

24

and cast you out of my life. I come against wondering spirit and distractions, I arrest you today by the power in the name of Jesus Christ, I bind you and cast you out of my life.

Today I receive the anointing to pray and get results, my prayers cannot be hindered nor delayed because Jesus is my Lord, I will pray today and get the desired results, I decree open heavens upon my prayers. I baptize myself in the fire of the Holy Ghost, so I have become too hot for the enemy to handle. My prayers today will attract divine intervention to every situation in my life; signs and wonders will follow my prayers today, testimonies will follow my prayers today and the name of God alone will be glorified, in Jesus name. Amen!

PRAYER POINTS

1. O God my Father, thank you for being my God, my Father and my friend.
2. O God my Father, thank for the privilege to know you and the power of the resurrection of Jesus Christ.
3. O God my Father, thank you for always being there for me and with me.
4. O God my Father, thank you for the great and mighty things that you are doing in my life.
5. O God my Father, thank you for your provision and protection over me and my household.
6. O God my Father, thank you for always answering my prayers.
7. I confess my sins before you today and I ask you to forgive me on the basis of your mercy, in the name of Jesus Christ.

8. Wash me clean today O Lord by the blood of Jesus Christ.

9. I cover myself and my household with the blood of Jesus Christ.

10. My prayers today will not be in vain; my prayers will produce the desired results in the name of Jesus Christ.

11. O God my Father, let every decision of the enemy against me be overturned in the name of Jesus Christ.

12. O God my Father, arise and re-arrange my life to fit into your divine plan, in the name of Jesus Christ.

13. O God my Father, arise and re-arrange my life to show forth your glory, in the name of Jesus Christ.

14. O God my Father, arise and re-arrange my life to fit into your divine progress set for me, in the name of Jesus Christ.

15. O God my Father, arise and re-arrange my life to fit into your divine favor set for me, in the name of Jesus Christ.

16. O God my Father, arise and re-arrange my life to receive miracles, in the name of Jesus Christ.

17. O God arise, re-arrange my life and prepare me for great achievements this month, in the name of Jesus Christ.

18. By the power in the name of Jesus Christ, I receive divine strength to pursue, overtake and recover my stolen blessings.

19. By the power in the name of Jesus Christ, I receive divine strength to pursue, overtake and recover my stolen miracles.

20. By the power in the name of Jesus Christ, I receive divine strength to pursue, overtake and recover my prosperity from the hands of the household wickedness.

21. By the power in the name of Jesus Christ, I receive divine strength to pursue, overtake and recover my

breakthroughs from the hands of principalities and powers.

22. Every curse of "thou shall not excel" issued against me, break today by the power in the blood of Jesus Christ.

23. Every curse of "thou shall not make it" issued against me, break today by the power in the blood of Jesus Christ.

24. Every curse of "thou shall not prosper" issued against me, break today by the power in the blood of Jesus Christ.

25. Every curse of "thou shall not live long" issued against me, break today by the power in the blood of Jesus Christ.

26. Every curse of "thou shall not progress" issued against me, break today by the power in the blood of Jesus Christ.

27. Every curse of "thou shall not eat the fruits of thy labor" issued against me, break today by the power in the blood of Jesus Christ.

28. Every curse of "thou shall not rejoice" issued against me, break today by the power in the blood of Jesus Christ.

29. Every curse of "hard labor less blessing" issued against me, break today by the power in the blood of Jesus Christ.

30. Every curse of "failure at the point of breakthrough" issued against me, break by the power in the blood of Jesus Christ.

31. O God my Father, arise and cancel every evil pronouncement against my life, in the name of Jesus Christ.

32. O God my Father, arise and cancel every evil pronouncement against my future, in the name of Jesus Christ.
33. O God my Father, arise and cancel every evil pronouncement against my finances, in the name of Jesus Christ.
34. O God my Father, arise and cancel every evil pronouncement against my family, in the name of Jesus Christ.
35. O God my Father, arise and cancel every evil pronouncement against the works of my hands, in the name of Jesus Christ.
36. The negative history of my family trying to destroy my life, you will not succeed, in the name of Jesus Christ.
37. The negative history of my family that has been hindering my blessings, be replaced today with uncommon favor, in the name of Jesus Christ.
38. The negative history of my family that has been keeping my helpers away, be replaced today with uncommon favor, in the name of Jesus Christ.
39. The negative history of my family that has been making it difficult for me to excel, be replaced today with uncommon success, in the name of Jesus Christ.
40. O God my Father, do something in my life today that will rewrite my family history, in the name of Jesus Christ.
41. Voice of darkness crying against me; be silenced forever, in the name of Jesus Christ.
42. Voice of witchcraft crying against me; be silenced forever, in the name of Jesus Christ.
43. Voice of household wickedness crying against me; be silenced forever, in the name of Jesus Christ.

44. Any evil meeting holding anywhere against me, scatter by the fire of God, in the name of Jesus Christ.
45. Any witchcraft meeting holding anywhere against me, scatter by the fire of God, in the name of Jesus Christ.
46. Demonic agents holding meetings to destroy me, arise today and begin to destroy yourselves; in the name of Jesus Christ.
47. Demonic agents holding meetings to attack my finances, arise today and begin to destroy yourselves; in the name of Jesus Christ.
48. Demonic agents holding meetings to make my life miserable, arise today and begin to destroy yourselves; in the name of Jesus Christ.
49. Demonic agents holding meetings to delay my miracles, arise today and begin to destroy yourselves; in the name of Jesus Christ.
50. Demonic agents holding meetings to hinder my prayers, arise today and begin to destroy yourselves; in the name of Jesus Christ.
51. Demonic agents holding meetings to attack my family, arise today and begin to destroy yourselves; in the name of Jesus Christ.
52. Demonic agents holding meetings to attack my marriage, arise today and begin to destroy yourselves; in the name of Jesus Christ.
53. Demonic agents holding meetings to change my destiny, arise today and begin to destroy yourselves; in the name of Jesus Christ.
54. Demonic agents holding meetings to destroy my future, arise today and begin to destroy yourselves; in the name of Jesus Christ.

55. Demonic agents holding meetings to change the plan of God for my life, arise today and begin to destroy yourselves; in the name of Jesus Christ.

56. Any power anywhere standing against my financial freedom; be destroyed today by thunder and the whirlwind of God, in the name of Jesus Christ.

57. Any power anywhere standing against my breakthrough; be destroyed today by thunder and the whirlwind of God, in the name of Jesus Christ.

58. Any power anywhere standing against my promotion; be destroyed today by thunder and the whirlwind of God, in the name of Jesus Christ.

59. Any power anywhere standing against my open heavens; be destroyed today thunder and the whirlwind of God, in the name of Jesus Christ.

60. Any power anywhere standing against my progress; be destroyed today by thunder and the whirlwind of God in the name of Jesus Christ.

61. My blessings, what are you doing in the camp of the enemy; come out now by the fire of God.

62. My greatness, what are you doing in the camp of the enemy; come out now by the fire of God.

63. My financial freedom, what are you doing in the camp of the enemy; come out now by the fire of God.

64. My answered prayers, what are you doing in the camp of the enemy; come out now by the fire of God.

65. My miracles, what are you doing in the camp of the enemy; come out now by the fire of God.

66. My breakthroughs, what are doing in the camp of the enemy; come out now by the fire of God.

67. My promotion, what are you doing in the camp of the enemy; come out now by the fire of God.

68. My joy, what are you doing in the camp of the enemy; come out now by the fire of God.
69. My testimonies, what are you doing in the camp of the enemy; come out now by the fire of God.
70. Solution to my problems, what are you doing in the camp of the enemy; come out now by the fire of God.
71. My fulfilled promises of God, what are you doing in the camp of the enemy; come out now by the fire of God.
72. My divine fruitfulness, what are you doing in the camp of the enemy; come out now by the fire of God.
73. My healing, what are you doing in the camp of the enemy; come out now by the fire of God.
74. My prosperity, what are you doing in the camp of the enemy; come out now by the fire of God.
75. Anything in my life that witchcraft agents have turned upside-down; be reversed by the fire of God, in the name of Jesus Christ.
76. Anything in my home that witchcraft agents have turned upside-down; be reversed by the fire of God, in the name of Jesus Christ.
77. Anything in my marriage that witchcraft agents have turned upside-down; be reversed by the fire of God, in the name of Jesus Christ.
78. Anything in my business that witchcraft agents have turned upside-down; be reversed by the fire of God, in the name of Jesus Christ.
79. Anything in my ministry that witchcraft agents have turned upside-down; be reversed by the fire of God, in the name of Jesus Christ.
80. Anything in my church that witchcraft agents have turned upside-down; be reversed by the fire of God, in the name of Jesus Christ.

81. Anything in my neighborhood that witchcraft agents have turned upside-down; be reversed by the fire of God, in the name of Jesus Christ.

82. By the power in the blood of Jesus Christ, I withdraw my money from the witchcraft bank account, in the name of Jesus Christ.

83. By the power in the blood of Jesus Christ, I stop the direct deposit of my income into the witchcraft bank account, in the name of Jesus Christ.

84. By the power in the blood of Jesus Christ, I stop the direct deposit of my income into the household wickedness bank account, in the name of Jesus Christ.

85. By the power in the name of Jesus Christ, I stop the direct deposit of my income into the hands of the devourer, in the name of Jesus Christ.

I cover my prayers in the blood of Jesus Christ. According to the Word of God, I have asked; I shall receive. I have knocked the door; it shall be opened unto me. I have sought; I shall find, in the name of Jesus Christ. It is written, "... Decree a thing, and it shall be established". As I have spoken in prayer, it shall be so. My prayers shall produce desired results. My prayers shall produce desired miracles. My prayers shall produce desired testimonies, in the name of Jesus Christ. Territorial spirit and power cannot hinder this prayer. Sins and flesh cannot hinder this prayer. It is done. It is sealed by the blood of Jesus Christ. It is delivered to me, in Jesus mighty name. Amen!

DAY THREE

INVADING DEMONIC INTELLIGENCE AGENCY

Passages To Read Before You Pray:
Job 5:12, Isaiah 8:9-10, Obadiah 1:17, Matthew 16:19,
Psalms 35, 3, 109, 68

In the book of Job 22:28, the Scripture says when I decree a thing, it shall be established for me. I stand on this Scripture and decree. I have come into the presence of God today to plead my case. I enter through the gate of praise, into the sanctuary of heaven. I cover myself in the precious blood of Jesus Christ. I baptize myself in the fire of the Holy Ghost. I charge this atmosphere with the fire of God, and I take this neighborhood for the Lord. I arrest every principality and power, territorial spirit, and every throne and kingdom that is not of God. I cast you down and I command you never to lift yourself up against me, because I have the life of God in me.

In the name of Jesus Christ, I confess my sins today, and I ask you O Lord to forgive me on the basis of your mercy. With all my heart, I forgive those who have sinned against me; from the past through this moment. I release them from any form of guilt and shame, in the name of Jesus Christ. I hereby plead the blood of Jesus over any sins committed by my parents and ancestors. I cancel through the Blood of Jesus Christ, any satanic covenants, exchanges, vows or transactions, made over my life, body, soul, spirit, and circumstances, in the name of Jesus Christ. I cancel every legal right that the devil may have against me, by the blood of Jesus Christ. The accuser of the brethren will have nothing against me, as I come to the presence of God in prayer.

The devil cannot hinder or delay my prayer, because I know who I am. I am a child of the Kingdom. I am a king and priest of the Lord, redeemed from the hand of the devil by the blood of Jesus Christ. I walk in power. I walk in miracle. Proverbs 18:21 says, death and life are in the power of my tongue; I command the power in my tongue to manifest now. I command my tongue to become fire, to consume all the powers of darkness in the air, the land, the sea, and beneath the earth. I hereby raise Holy Ghost standard against the prince of the power of the air and all the hosts of darkness in the air. I raise Holy Ghost standard against the queen of the coasts and all the hosts of darkness on the land. I raise Holy Ghost standard against the marine kingdom and all the hosts of darkness in the sea. I raise Holy Ghost standard against the kingdom of hell and all the hosts of darkness beneath the earth. I shoot down all the networks of demons gathering to resist my prayers. I rebuke and bind all the controlling forces of darkness standing against my prayers.

I declare that all satanic thrones, altars, dominions, principalities, powers, rulers of darkness, queens of the coast, queens of heavens, household wickedness, spiritual hosts of wickedness and all satanic works, have no power or authority over my life. I declare that satanic harassment and intimidation have no effect on me.

Today, I receive divine strength to pray; I will not pray in vain. I will not pray amiss. My prayers will bring the desired results. I command the fountain of prayer to open now, and to flow into my life, I command the warring angels of God to descend and fight on my behalf. Every minute and every hour that I spend in prayer, will bring solution. Every prayer point will attract divine attention and divine intervention. I decree open heavens over my prayers, and today, God of heaven and earth will attend to my case. My prayers today will shake the heavens and move the earth. Testimonies, miracles, healings, breakthroughs, and signs and wonders, will follow my prayers. At the end of this prayer session, my life will never be the same again.

PRAYER POINTS

1. O God my Father, thank you for being my God, my Father and my friend.
2. O God my Father, thank you for the privilege to know you and the power of the resurrection of Jesus Christ.
3. O God my Father, thank you for always being there for me and with me.
4. O God my Father, thank you for the great and mighty things that you are doing in my life.
5. O God my Father, thank you for your provision and protection over me and my household.
6. O God my Father, thank you for always answering my prayers.
7. I confess my sins before you today and I ask you to forgive me on the basis of your mercy, in the name of Jesus Christ.
8. Wash me clean today O Lord by the blood of Jesus Christ.
9. I cover myself and my household with the blood of Jesus Christ.
10. My prayers today will not go in vain; my prayers will produce the desired results in the name of Jesus Christ.
11. O God my Father, let the plan and agenda of the wicked against my life be exposed, in the name of Jesus Christ.

12. O God my Father, let the plan and agenda of the wicked against my ministry be exposed, in the name of Jesus Christ.

13. O God my Father, let the plan and agenda of the wicked against my marriage be exposed, in the name of Jesus Christ.

14. O God my Father, let the plan and agenda of the wicked against my family be exposed, in the name of Jesus Christ.

15. O God my Father, let the plan and agenda of the wicked against my job be exposed, in the name of Jesus Christ.

16. O God my Father, let the plan and agenda of the wicked against my business be exposed, in the name of Jesus Christ.

17. O God my Father, let the plan and agenda of the wicked against my children be exposed, in the name of Jesus Christ.

18. O God my Father, let the plan and agenda of the wicked against my spouse be exposed, in the name of Jesus Christ.

19. O God my Father, let the plan and agenda of the wicked against my finances be exposed, in the name of Jesus Christ.

20. O God my Father, let the plan and agenda of the wicked against my future be exposed, in the name of Jesus Christ.

21. O God my Father, let the plan and agenda of the wicked against my divine purpose be exposed, in the name of Jesus Christ.

22. I release confusion into the headquarters of demonic intelligence agency working against me, in the name of Jesus Christ.

23. I release confusion into the headquarters of demonic intelligence agency working against my family, in the name of Jesus Christ.
24. I release confusion into the headquarters of demonic intelligence agency working against my marriage, in the name of Jesus Christ.
25. I release confusion into the headquarters of demonic intelligence agency working against my spouse, in the name of Jesus Christ.
26. I release confusion into the headquarters of demonic intelligence agency working against my children, in the name of Jesus Christ.
27. I release confusion into the headquarters of demonic intelligence agency working against my destiny, in the name of Jesus Christ.
28. I release confusion into the headquarters of demonic intelligence agency working against my finances, in the name of Jesus Christ.
29. I release confusion into the headquarters of demonic intelligence agency working against my business, in the name of Jesus Christ.
30. I release confusion into the headquarters of demonic intelligence agency working against my spiritual life, in the name of Jesus Christ.
31. I release confusion into the headquarters of demonic intelligence agency working against my ministry, in the name of Jesus Christ.
32. I release confusion into the headquarters of demonic intelligence agency working against answers to my prayers, in the name of Jesus Christ.

33. I release confusion into the headquarters of demonic intelligence agency working against my good efforts, in the name of Jesus Christ.

34. I release confusion into the headquarters of demonic intelligence agency working against my progress, in the name of Jesus Christ.

35. I release confusion into the headquarters of demonic intelligence agency working against my future, in the name of Jesus Christ.

36. I release confusion into the headquarters of demonic intelligence agency working against my divine purpose, in the name of Jesus Christ.

37. I render all the efforts of demonic intelligence agents useless over my life, in the name of Jesus Christ.

38. I render all the efforts of demonic intelligence agents useless over my marriage, in the name of Jesus Christ.

39. I render all the efforts of demonic intelligence agents useless over my family, in the name of Jesus Christ.

40. I render all the efforts of demonic intelligence agents useless over my ministry, in the name of Jesus Christ.

41. I render all the efforts of demonic intelligence agents useless over my spouse, in the name of Jesus Christ.

42. I render all the efforts of demonic intelligence agents useless over my children, in the name of Jesus Christ.

43. I render all the efforts of demonic intelligence agents useless over my future, in the name of Jesus Christ.

44. I arrest every demonic intelligence agent monitoring my life, in the name of Jesus Christ.

45. I arrest every demonic intelligence agent monitoring my movement, in the name of Jesus Christ.

46. I arrest every demonic intelligence agent monitoring my destiny, in the name of Jesus Christ.

47. I arrest every demonic intelligence agent monitoring my family, in the name of Jesus Christ.

48. I arrest every demonic intelligence agent monitoring my prayer life, in the name of Jesus Christ.

49. I arrest every demonic intelligence agent monitoring my finances, in the name of Jesus Christ.

50. I arrest every demonic intelligence agent monitoring my bank account, in the name of Jesus Christ.

51. I arrest every demonic intelligence agent monitoring my sources of income, in the name of Jesus Christ.

52. I arrest every demonic intelligence agent monitoring my progress, in the name of Jesus Christ.

53. I arrest every demonic intelligence agent monitoring my health, in the name of Jesus Christ.

54. I arrest every demonic intelligence agent monitoring what God is doing in my life, in the name of Jesus Christ.

55. I arrest every demonic intelligence agent monitoring my ministry, in the name of Jesus Christ.

56. I arrest every demonic intelligence agent monitoring my spiritual life, in the name of Jesus Christ.

57. I release heavenly atomic bomb upon the headquarters of demonic intelligence agency that refuses to let me live the life that God had designed for me, in the name of Jesus Christ.

58. I release heavenly atomic bomb upon the headquarters of demonic intelligence agency that refuses to let me enjoy my marriage, in the name of Jesus Christ.

59. I release heavenly atomic bomb upon the headquarters of demonic intelligence agency that refuses to let me enjoy the goodness of the Lord in the land of the living, in the name of Jesus Christ.

60. I release heavenly atomic bomb upon the headquarters of demonic intelligence agency that refuses to let me enjoy the blessings of God prepared for me, in the name of Jesus Christ.

61. I release heavenly atomic bomb upon the headquarters of demonic intelligence agency that refuses to let me enjoy answers to my prayers, in the name of Jesus Christ.

62. I pronounce divine judgment against every satanic spy assigned against me, in the name of Jesus Christ.

63. I pronounce divine judgment against every satanic spy assigned against my marriage, in the name of Jesus Christ.

64. I pronounce divine judgment against every satanic spy assigned against my spiritual life, in the name of Jesus Christ.

65. I pronounce divine judgment against every satanic spy assigned against my ministry, in the name of Jesus Christ.

66. I pronounce divine judgment against every monitoring spirit working against me, in the name of Jesus Christ.

I cover my prayers in the blood of Jesus Christ. According to the Word of God, I have asked; I shall receive. I have knocked the door; it shall be opened unto me. I have sought; I shall find, in the name of Jesus Christ. It is written, "… Decree a thing, and it shall be established". As I have spoken in prayer, it shall be so. My prayers shall produce desired results. My prayers shall produce desired miracles. My prayers shall produce desired testimonies, in the name of Jesus Christ. Territorial spirit and power cannot hinder this prayer. Sins and flesh cannot hinder this prayer. It is done. It is sealed by the blood of Jesus Christ. It is delivered to me, in Jesus mighty name. Amen!

DAY FOUR

JEZEBEL MUST BE STOPPED

Passages To Read Before You Pray:
Jeremiah 1:10, Jeremiah 51:20, Exodus 22:18,
2 Kings 9:1-37

In the book of Job 22:28, the Scripture says when I decree a thing, it shall be established for me. I stand on this Scripture and decree. I have come into the presence of God today to plead my case. I enter through the gate of praise into the sanctuary of heaven. I cover myself in the precious blood of Jesus Christ. I baptize myself in the fire of the Holy Ghost. I charge this atmosphere with the fire of God, and I take this neighborhood for the Lord. I arrest every principality and power, territorial spirit, and every throne and kingdom that is not of God. I cast you down and I command you never to lift yourself up against me, because I have the life of God in me.

In the name of Jesus Christ, I confess my sins today, and I ask you O Lord to forgive me on the basis of your mercy. With all my heart, I forgive those who have sinned against me from the past through this moment. I release them from any form of guilt and shame, in the name of Jesus Christ. I hereby plead the blood of Jesus over any sins committed by my parents and ancestors. I cancel through the Blood of Jesus Christ, any satanic covenants, exchanges, vows or transactions made over my life, body, soul, spirit, and circumstances, in the name of Jesus Christ. I cancel every legal right that the devil may have against me, by the blood of Jesus Christ. The accuser of the brethren will have nothing against me as I come to the presence of God in prayer.

The devil cannot hinder or delay my prayer, because I know who I am. I am a child of the Kingdom; I am a king and priest of the Lord, redeemed from the hand of the devil by the blood of Jesus Christ. I declare that all satanic thrones, altars, dominions, principalities, powers, rulers of darkness, queen of the coast, queen of heavens, household wickedness, spiritual hosts of wickedness and all satanic works, have no power or authority over my life. I declare that satanic harassment and intimidation have no effect on me.

Today I receive divine strength to pray; I will not pray in vain. I will not pray amiss. My prayers will bring the desired results. I command the fountain of prayer to open now, and flow into my life, I command the warring angels of God to descend and fight on my behalf. Every minute and every hour that I spend in prayer will bring solution. Every prayer point will attract divine attention and divine intervention. I decree open heavens over my prayers, and today, God of heaven and earth will attend to my case. My prayers today will shake the heavens and move the earth; testimonies, miracles, healing, breakthrough, signs and wonders will follow my prayers. At the end of this prayer session, my life will never be the same again.

PRAYER POINTS

1. O God my Father, thank you for being my God, my Father and my friend.
2. O God my Father, thank you for the privilege to know you and the power of the resurrection of Jesus Christ.
3. O God my Father, thank you for always being there for me and with me.

4. O God my Father, thank you for the great and mighty things that you are doing in my life.
5. O God my Father, thank you for your provision and protection over me and my household.
6. O God my Father, thank you for always answering my prayers.
7. I confess my sins before you today and I ask you to forgive me on the basis of your mercy, in the name of Jesus Christ.
8. Wash me clean today O Lord by the blood of Jesus Christ.
9. I cover myself and my household with the blood of Jesus Christ.
10. My prayers today will not go in vain; my prayers will produce the desired results in the name of Jesus Christ.
11. By the authority in the name of Jesus Christ, I root out any evil establishment working against me.
12. By the authority in the name of Jesus Christ, I root out every evil establishment working against my family.
13. By the authority in the name of Jesus Christ, I root out every evil establishment working against my destiny.
14. By the authority in the name of Jesus Christ, I root out every evil establishment working against my marriage.
15. By the authority in the name of Jesus Christ, I root out every evil establishment working against my ministry.
16. By the power in the blood of Jesus Christ, I pull down every stronghold built against my life, in the name of Jesus Christ.
17. By the power in the blood of Jesus Christ, I pull down every stronghold built against my family, in the name of Jesus Christ.

18. By the power in the blood of Jesus Christ, I pull down every stronghold built against my marriage in the name of Jesus Christ.

19. By the power in the blood of Jesus Christ, I pull down every stronghold built against my finances in the name of Jesus Christ.

20. By the power in the blood of Jesus Christ, I pull down every stronghold built against my ministry in the name of Jesus Christ.

21. As God's weapon of war, I destroy today every work of the devil manifesting in my life, in the name of Jesus Christ.

22. As God's weapon of war, I destroy today every work of the devil manifesting in my business, in the name of Jesus Christ.

23. As God's weapon of war, I destroy today every work of the devil manifesting in my home, in the name of Jesus Christ.

24. As God's weapon of war, I destroy today every work of the devil manifesting in my finances, in the name of Jesus Christ.

25. As God's weapon of war, I destroy today every work of the devil manifesting in the life of my spouse, in the name of Jesus Christ.

26. As God's weapon of war, I destroy today every work of the devil manifesting in the life of my children, in the name of Jesus Christ.

27. As God's weapon of war, I crush the throne of Ahab erected in my life, in the name of Jesus Christ.

28. As God's weapon of war, I crush the throne of Jezebel erected against me, in the name of Jesus Christ.

29. By the authority in the name of Jesus Christ, I decree today, Jezebel of my life must die.
30. By the authority in the name of Jesus Christ, I decree today, Ahab of my life must die.
31. By the authority in the name of Jesus Christ, I decree today, my Goliath must die.
32. By the authority in the name of Jesus Christ, I decree today, my Pharaoh must die.
33. By the authority in the name of Jesus Christ, I decree today, my Herod must die.
34. O God my Father, let Jehu's anointing fall upon me today, in the name of Jesus Christ.
35. O God my Father, let the anointing that tolerates no nonsense fall upon me now, in the name of Jesus Christ.
36. O God my Father, let the anointing that tolerates no evil fall upon me now, in the name of Jesus Christ.
37. O God my Father, let the anointing upon my life destroy my Ahab today, in the name of Jesus Christ.
38. O God my Father, let the anointing upon my life destroy my Jezebel today, in the name of Jesus Christ.
39. Today, I receive a mandate to crush the house of Jezebel, and they shall not escape the wrath of God, in the name of Jesus Christ.
40. Today, I receive a mandate to crush the house of Ahab, and they shall not escape the wrath of God, in the name of Jesus Christ.
41. O God arise and avenge me of Jezebel and her kingdom that has been working against me, in the name of Jesus Christ.
42. O God my Father, let the entire house of Ahab working against me perish, at the mention of the name of Jesus Christ.

43. O God my Father, let the entire kingdom of Jezebel working against me perish at the mention of your name, in the name of Jesus Christ.

44. O God my Father, let the entire kingdom of Jezebel working against my family perish at the mention of your name, in the name of Jesus Christ.

45. O God my Father, let the entire kingdom of Jezebel working against my destiny perish, at the mention of the name of Jesus Christ.

46. O God my Father, let the entire kingdom of Jezebel working against my finances perish, at the mention of the name of Jesus Christ.

47. O God my Father, let the entire kingdom of Jezebel working against my marriage perish, at the mention of the name of Jesus Christ.

48. Today, my Jezebel will die and have no burying place, in the name of Jesus Christ.

49. O God my Father, let my Jezebel be put to an open shame, in the name of Jesus Christ.

50. O God my Father, let my Jezebel die a shameful death, in the name of Jesus Christ.

51. Today, I receive the mantle of Jehu to destroy the house of Jezebel by the power of prayer, in the name of Jesus Christ.

52. Today, I receive the zeal of Jehu to destroy the house of Jezebel by the power of prayer, in the name of Jesus Christ.

53. O God my Father, send the heavenly chariots of fire to run through and destroy the camp of my enemy, in the name of Jesus Christ.

54. Today, I nullify every witchcraft practice against me by the Jezebel spirit, in the name of Jesus Christ.

55. Today I nullify every manipulation used against me by Jezebel spirit, in the name of Jesus Christ.
56. O God my Father, let every conspiracy of Jezebel to steal my inheritance be scattered, in the name of Jesus Christ.
57. O God my Father, let every accusation of Jezebel to destroy my reputation be nullified, in the name of Jesus Christ.
58. O God my Father, let Jezebel's control over my life be nullified and become useless, in the name of Jesus Christ.

I cover my prayers in the blood of Jesus Christ. According to the Word of God, I have asked, I shall receive. I have knocked the door, it shall be opened unto me. I have sought, I shall find, in the name of Jesus Christ. It is written, "... Decree a thing, and it shall be established". As I have spoken in prayer, it shall be so. My prayers shall produce desire results. My prayers shall produce desired miracles. My prayers shall produce desired testimonies, in the name of Jesus Christ. Territorial spirit and power cannot hinder this prayer. Sins and flesh cannot hinder this prayer. It is done. It is sealed by the blood of Jesus Christ. It is delivered to me, in Jesus might name. Amen!

DAY FIVE

STRATEGIC WARFARE PRAYERS

Passages To Read Before You Pray:
1 Samuel 5:1-12, Revelation 12:11, 2 Chronicles 20:1-29,
Psalms 109, 55, 35

In the book of Job 22:28, the Scripture says when I decree a thing, it shall be established for me. I stand on this Scripture and decree. I have come into the presence of God today to plead my case. I enter through the gate of praise into the sanctuary of heaven. I cover myself in the precious blood of Jesus Christ. I baptize myself in the fire of the Holy Ghost. I charge this atmosphere with the fire of God, and I take this neighborhood for the Lord. I arrest every principality and power, territorial spirit, and every throne and kingdom that is not of God. I cast you down and I command you never to lift yourself up against me, because I have the life of God in me.

In the name of Jesus Christ, I confess my sins today, and I ask you O Lord to forgive me on the basis of your mercy. With all my heart, I forgive those who have sinned against me from the past through this moment. I release them from any form of guilt and shame, in the name of Jesus Christ. I hereby plead the blood of Jesus over any sins committed by my parents and ancestors. I cancel through the Blood of Jesus Christ, any satanic covenants, exchanges, vows or transactions made over my life, body, soul, spirit, and circumstances, in the name of Jesus Christ. I cancel every legal right that the devil may have against me, by the blood of Jesus Christ. The accuser of the brethren will have nothing against me as I come to the presence of God in prayer.

The devil cannot hinder or delay my prayer, because I know who I am. I am a child of the Kingdom; I am a king and priest of the Lord, redeemed from the hand of the devil by the blood of Jesus Christ. I declare that all satanic thrones, altars, dominions, principalities, powers, rulers of darkness, queen of the coast, queen of heavens, household wickedness, spiritual hosts of wickedness and all satanic works, have no power or authority over my life. I declare that satanic harassment and intimidation have no effect on me.

Today I receive divine strength to pray; I will not pray in vain. I will not pray amiss. My prayers will bring the desired results. I command the fountain of prayer to open now, and flow into my life, I command the warring angels of God to descend and fight on my behalf. Every minute and every hour that I spend in prayer will bring solution. Every prayer point will attract divine attention and divine intervention. I decree open heavens over my prayers, and today, God of heaven and earth will attend to my case. My prayers today will shake the heavens and move the earth; testimonies, miracles, healing, breakthrough, signs and wonders will follow my prayers. At the end of this prayer session, my life will never be the same again.

PRAYER POINTS

1. O God my Father, thank you for being my God, my Father and my friend.
2. O God my Father, thank you for the privilege to know you and the power of the resurrection of Jesus Christ.
3. O God my Father, thank you for always being there for me and with me.

4. O God my Father, thank you for the great and mighty things that you are doing in my life.
5. O God my Father, thank you for your provision and protection over me and my household.
6. O God my Father, thank you for always answering my prayers.
7. I confess my sins before you today and I ask you to forgive me on the basis of your mercy, in the name of Jesus Christ.
8. Wash me clean today O Lord by the blood of Jesus Christ.
9. I cover myself and my household with the blood of Jesus Christ.
10. My prayers today will not go in vain; my prayers will produce the desired results in the name of Jesus Christ.
11. I soak myself in the blood of Jesus Christ.
12. I baptize myself in the fire of the Holy Ghost, in the name of Jesus Christ.
13. I stand on the Word of God. I decree today that any agent of darkness assigned to handle my case will not live to see another day, in the name of Jesus Christ.
14. O God my Father, let my life become the Ark of the Covenant, and let my life bring total destruction upon anyone who wants to trouble me, in the name of Jesus Christ.
15. O God my Father, let my life become the Ark of the Covenant, and let destruction fall upon any power anywhere attacking me in my dream, in the name of Jesus Christ.
16. O God my Father, let my life become the Ark of the Covenant, and let destruction fall upon any power

anywhere assigned to enslave me, in the name of Jesus Christ.

17. O God my Father, let my life become the Ark of the Covenant, and let total destruction fall upon any power anywhere attacking my finances, in the name of Jesus Christ.

18. O God my Father, let my family become the Ark of the Covenant, and let total destruction fall upon any power that wants to trouble us, in the name of Jesus Christ.

19. Any power anywhere waiting for me to make a mistake that will cost me my life; today, I decree that you will die in my place, in the name of Jesus Christ.

20. Any agent of darkness planning to take my children's lives to use as an extension of his/her life, you are a liar. My children are untouchable; my children are covered in the blood of Jesus. Your time is up, and it is time for you to die, in the name of Jesus Christ.

21. Any agent of darkness planning to take my spouse's life to use as an extension of his/her life, you are a liar. My spouse is untouchable; he/she is covered in the blood of Jesus. Your time is up and it is time for you to die, in the name of Jesus Christ.

22. Any power anywhere laid in ambush for me, in order to do me evil, I release the fire of God to destroy you and your armies, in the name of Jesus Christ.

23. Any power anywhere laid in ambush for me, in order to rob me of my blessings; I release the fire of God to destroy you and your armies, in the name of Jesus Christ.

24. Any power anywhere laid in ambush for me, in order to rob me of my miracles, I release the fire of God to

destroy you and your armies, in the name of Jesus Christ.

25. Every agent of darkness harassing me in my place of work, you will not escape the judgment of God, in the name of Jesus Christ.

26. By the power and authority in the name of Jesus Christ, I come against satanic harassment; everyone involved will not escape the judgment of God, in the name of Jesus Christ.

27. By the authority and power in the blood of Jesus Christ, I come against satanic intimidation; everyone involved will not escape the judgment of God, in the name of Jesus Christ.

28. Any agent of darkness planning to take my life and to use as an extension of his/her life, you are a liar. I am untouchable; I have the life of God in me, your time is up and it is time for you to die, in the name of Jesus Christ.

29. I release the consuming fire of God to scatter and destroy every local network of darkness working against me; you cannot regroup again. It's all over, in the name of Jesus Christ.

30. I release the consuming fire of God to scatter and destroy every local network of darkness working against my family; you cannot regroup again. It's all over, in the name of Jesus Christ.

31. I release the consuming fire of God to scatter and destroy every local network of darkness working against my finances; you cannot regroup again. It's all over, in the name of Jesus Christ.

32. I release the consuming fire of God to scatter and destroy every local network of darkness working against

my breakthrough; you cannot regroup again. It's all over, in the name of Jesus Christ.

33. I release the consuming fire of God to scatter and destroy every local network of darkness working against my success; you cannot regroup again. It's all over, in the name of Jesus Christ.

34. I release the consuming fire of God to scatter and destroy every regional network of darkness working against me; you cannot regroup again. It's all over, in the name of Jesus Christ.

35. I release the consuming fire of God to scatter and destroy every regional network of darkness working against my family; you cannot regroup again. It's all over, in the name of Jesus Christ.

36. I release the consuming fire of God to scatter and destroy every regional network of darkness working against my breakthrough; you cannot regroup again. It's all over, in the name of Jesus Christ.

37. I release the consuming fire of God to scatter and destroy every regional network of darkness working against my finances; you cannot regroup again. It's all over, in the name of Jesus Christ.

38. I release the consuming fire of God to scatter and destroy every regional network of darkness working against my success; you cannot regroup again. It's all over, in the name of Jesus Christ.

39. I release the consuming fire of God to scatter and destroy every national network of darkness working against me; you cannot regroup again. It's all over, in the name of Jesus Christ.

40. I release the consuming fire of God to scatter and destroy every national network of darkness working

against my family; you cannot regroup again. It's all over, in the name of Jesus Christ.

41. I release the consuming fire of God to scatter and destroy every national network of darkness working against my finances; you cannot regroup again. It's all over, in the name of Jesus Christ.

42. I release the consuming fire of God to scatter and destroy every national network of darkness working against my breakthrough; you cannot regroup again. It's all over, in the name of Jesus Christ.

43. I release the consuming fire of God to scatter and destroy every national network of darkness working against my success; you cannot regroup again. It's all over, in the name of Jesus Christ.

44. I release the consuming fire of God to scatter and destroy every global network of darkness working against me; you cannot regroup again. It's all over, in the name of Jesus Christ.

45. I release the consuming fire of God to scatter and destroy every global network of darkness working against my family; you cannot regroup again. It's all over, in the name of Jesus Christ.

46. I release the consuming fire of God to scatter and destroy every global network of darkness working against my finances; you cannot regroup again. It's all over, in the name of Jesus Christ.

47. I release the consuming fire of God to scatter and destroy every global network of darkness working against my breakthrough; you cannot regroup again. It's all over, in the name of Jesus Christ.

48. I release the consuming fire of God to scatter and destroy every global network of darkness working

against my success; you cannot regroup again. It's all over, in the name of Jesus Christ.

49. By the authority and power in the blood of Jesus, I unseat every power of darkness sitting on my breakthroughs, in the name of Jesus Christ.

50. By the authority and power in the blood of Jesus, I unseat every power of darkness sitting on my success, in the name of Jesus Christ.

51. By the authority and power in the blood of Jesus, I unseat every power of darkness sitting on my finances, in the name of Jesus Christ.

52. By the authority and power in the blood of Jesus, I unseat every power of darkness sitting on my promotion, in the name of Jesus Christ.

53. By the authority and power in the blood of Jesus, I unseat every power of darkness sitting on my glory, in the name of Jesus Christ.

54. By the authority and power in the blood of Jesus, I unseat every power of darkness sitting on my financial freedom, in the name of Jesus Christ.

55. By the authority and power in the blood of Jesus, I unseat every power of darkness sitting on my business breakthroughs, in the name of Jesus Christ.

56. O God my Father, lunch a surprise attack against the camp of my enemies. Let there be complete destruction in the camp of my enemy, in the name of Jesus Christ.

57. O God my Father, let not my enemies survive the divine assault against me, in the name of Jesus Christ.

58. O God my Father, let the armies of heaven locate and completely destroy hidden camps of my enemies, in the name of Jesus Christ.

59. O God my Father, this battle has been going on for too long; fight for me, put a quick end to this warfare, and let the outcome of this battle favor me, in the name of Jesus Christ.

60. By the blood of Jesus Christ, I claim victory over every battle of my life, in the name of Jesus Christ.

I cover my prayers in the blood of Jesus Christ. According to the Word of God, I have asked, I shall receive. I have knocked the door, it shall be opened unto me. I have sought, I shall find, in the name of Jesus Christ. It is written, "... Decree a thing, and it shall be established". As I have spoken in prayer, it shall be so. My prayers shall produce desire results. My prayers shall produce desired miracles. My prayers shall produce desired testimonies, in the name of Jesus Christ. Territorial spirit and power cannot hinder this prayer. Sins and flesh cannot hinder this prayer. It is done. It is sealed by the blood of Jesus Christ. It is delivered to me, in Jesus might name. Amen!

DAY SIX

PRAYER TO CANCEL EVIL TRANSACTION

Passages To Read Before You Pray:

John 2:13-17, I Corinthians 3:16-17, Psalms 83, 30, 86, 3,
Jeremiah 1:1-19

In the book of Job 22:28, the Scripture says when I decree a thing, it shall be established for me. I stand on this Scripture and decree. I have come today to fellowship with my heavenly Father, and make my requests and needs known unto Him. I cannot be hindered nor delayed because I know who I am in the Lord. I am a child of the Kingdom, born of the Spirit, redeemed by the blood of Jesus Christ. I walk in authority, living life without any apology because the power and authority has been given to me according to the Word of God in the book of Luke 9:1.

As I have come to pray today and to fellowship with my heavenly Father, I cover myself in the blood of Jesus Christ, and I put on the whole armor of God. I hereby come against every Prince of Persia that wants to hinder my prayer, I arrest you by the power in the blood of Jesus Christ, and I bind you and cast you down into the pit of hell.

I come against principalities and powers that wrestle with me and my prayers, I arrest you today by the power in the name of Jesus Christ, and I bind you and cast down into the pit of hell. I come against the rulers of the darkness of this world, against spiritual wickedness in high places, I arrest you all by the power in the name of Jesus Christ, and I bind you and cast you down into the pit of hell. I come against weakness and weariness, I arrest you today by the power in the name of Jesus Christ, and I bind you and cast you out of my life. I come against wondering spirit and distractions, I arrest you today by the power in the name of Jesus Christ, and I bind you and cast you out of my life.

Today I receive the anointing to pray and get results, my prayers cannot be hindered nor delayed because Jesus is my Lord, I will pray today and get the desired results, I decree open heavens upon my prayers. I baptize myself in the fire of the Holy Ghost; therefore I have become too hot for the enemy to handle. My prayers today will attract divine intervention to every situation in my life; signs and wonders will follow my prayers today, testimonies will follow my prayers today and the name of God alone will be glorified, in Jesus name. Amen!

PRAYER POINTS

1. O God my Father, thank you for being my God, my Father and my friend.
2. O God my Father, thank you for the privilege to know you and the power of the resurrection of Jesus Christ.
3. O God my Father, thank you for always being there for me and with me.
4. O God my Father, thank you for the great and mighty things that you are doing in my life.
5. O God my Father, thank you for your provision and protection over me and my household.
6. O God my Father, thank you for always answering my prayers.
7. I confess my sins before you today and I ask you to forgive me on the basis of your mercy, in the name of Jesus Christ.

8. Wash me clean today O Lord by the blood of Jesus Christ.

9. I cover myself and my household with the blood of Jesus Christ.

10. My prayers today will not go in vain; my prayers will produce the desired results in the name of Jesus Christ.

11. Every satanic trader buying and selling in my life, I bind you and cast you out of my life, by the power and authority in the name of Jesus Christ.

12. Any spirit or power buying and selling in my life, your time is up, come out with all your merchandise, in the name of Jesus Christ.

13. Any spirit or power trying to exchange my glory to something else, you are not allowed to tamper with my glory, in the name of Jesus Christ.

14. Any spirit or power trying to change my destiny to something else, you are not allowed to tamper with my destiny, in the name of Jesus Christ.

15. Any spirit or power trying to change my future to something else, you are not allowed to tamper with my future in the name of Jesus Christ.

16. Any spirit or power stealing my blessing to sell to profit, you are no longer allowed and you will not escape the judgment of God, in the name of Jesus Christ.

17. O God my Father, let my stolen blessings begin to torment them in the camp of my enemy, until they return it back to me, in the name of Jesus Christ.

18. Every satanic merchandise in my temple/life, I set you on fire, in the name of Jesus Christ.

19. Every satanic merchandise in the life of my spouse, I set you on fire, in the name of Jesus Christ.
20. Every satanic merchandise in the life of my children, I set you on fire, in the name of Jesus Christ.
21. Every satanic merchandise in my church, I set you on fire, in the name of Jesus Christ.
22. Every satanic merchandise in my home, I set you on fire, in the name of Jesus Christ.
23. O God my Father, let every evil transaction concerning my life be cancelled, in the name of Jesus Christ.
24. O God my Father, let every evil transaction concerning my spouse be cancelled, in the name of Jesus Christ.
25. O God my Father, let every evil transaction concerning my children be cancelled, in the name of Jesus Christ.
26. O God my Father, let every evil transaction concerning my marriage be cancelled, in the name of Jesus Christ.
27. O God my Father, let every evil transaction concerning my destiny be cancelled, in the name of Jesus Christ.
28. O God my Father, let every evil transaction concerning my future be cancelled, in the name of Jesus Christ.
29. O God my Father, let every evil transaction concerning my dreams be cancelled, in the name of Jesus Christ.
30. Satanic agent of change, you cannot change my destiny, my destiny is covered in the blood of Jesus Christ.

31. Satanic agent of change, you cannot change the destiny of my spouse, my spouse's destiny is covered in the blood of Jesus Christ.

32. Satanic agent of change, you cannot change my children's destiny, my children's destiny is covered in the blood of Jesus Christ.

33. Satanic agent of change, you cannot change the plan of God for my life, it is done and sealed by the blood of Jesus Christ.

34. Satanic agent of change, you cannot change my future, my future is in the hands of God, in the name of Jesus Christ.

35. Any power anywhere trying to turn my life into a shopping mall for the enemy, loose your hold upon my life now, in the name of Jesus Christ.

36. Any power anywhere trying to turn my life into a satanic drive through, you will not escape the judgment of God, in the name of Jesus Christ.

37. Today I drive out any spirit or power buying and selling in my life, in the name of Jesus Christ.

38. Today I drive out every satanic agent of change residing in my life, in the name of Jesus Christ.

39. Every satanic merchandise dumped in my life, I set it on fire, in the name of Jesus Christ.

40. O God my Father, let there be a total cleansing in every area of my life, in the name of Jesus Christ.

41. Today I overthrow every satanic establishment that is troubling my life, in the name of Jesus Christ.

42. Today I overthrow every satanic king and kingdom working against me, in the name of Jesus Christ.

43. Today I overthrow every satanic king and kingdom working against my marriage, in the name of Jesus Christ.

44. Today I overthrow every satanic king and kingdom working against my children, in the name of Jesus Christ.

45. Today I overthrow every satanic king and kingdom working against my progress, in the name of Jesus Christ.

46. Today I overthrow every satanic king and kingdom working against the will of God for my life, in the name of Jesus Christ.

I cover my prayers in the blood of Jesus Christ. According to the Word of God, I have asked; I shall receive. I have knocked the door; it shall be opened unto me. I have sought; I shall find, in the name of Jesus Christ. It is written, "... Decree a thing, and it shall be established". As I have spoken in prayer, it shall be so. My prayers shall produce desired results. My prayers shall produce desired miracles. My prayers shall produce desired testimonies, in the name of Jesus Christ. Territorial spirit and power cannot hinder this prayer. Sins and flesh cannot hinder this prayer. It is done. It is sealed by the blood of Jesus Christ. It is delivered to me, in Jesus mighty name. Amen!

DAY SEVEN

WAR AGAINST SATANIC CONTRACTORS

Passages To Read Before You Pray:
Numbers 22:1-12, Isaiah 8:9-10, Psalms 3, 2, 68, 83, 109

In the book of Job 22:28, the Scripture says when I decree a thing, it shall be established for me. I stand on this Scripture and decree. I have come into the presence of God today to plead my case. I enter through the gate of praise, into the sanctuary of heaven. I cover myself in the precious blood of Jesus Christ. I baptize myself in the fire of the Holy Ghost. I charge this atmosphere with the fire of God, and I take this neighborhood for the Lord. I arrest every principality and power, territorial spirit, and every throne and kingdom that is not of God. I cast you down and I command you never to lift yourself up against me, because I have the life of God in me.

In the name of Jesus Christ, I confess my sins today, and I ask you O Lord to forgive me on the basis of your mercy. With all my heart, I forgive those who have sinned against me; from the past through this moment. I release them from any form of guilt and shame, in the name of Jesus Christ. I hereby plead the blood of Jesus over any sins committed by my parents and ancestors. I cancel through the Blood of Jesus Christ, any satanic covenants, exchanges, vows or transactions, made over my life, body, soul, spirit, and circumstances, in the name of Jesus Christ. I cancel every legal right that the devil may have against me, by the blood of Jesus Christ. The accuser of the brethren will have nothing against me, as I come to the presence of God in prayer.

The devil cannot hinder or delay my prayer, because I know who I am. I am a child of the Kingdom. I am a king and priest of the

Lord, redeemed from the hand of the devil by the blood of Jesus Christ. I walk in power. I walk in miracle. Proverbs 18:21 says, death and life are in the power of my tongue; I command the power in my tongue to manifest now. I command my tongue to become fire, to consume all the powers of darkness in the air, the land, the sea, and beneath the earth. I hereby raise Holy Ghost standard against the prince of the power of the air and all the hosts of darkness in the air. I raise Holy Ghost standard against the queen of the coasts and all the hosts of darkness on the land. I raise Holy Ghost standard against the marine kingdom and all the hosts of darkness in the sea. I raise Holy Ghost standard against the kingdom of hell and all the hosts of darkness beneath the earth. I shoot down all the networks of demons gathering to resist my prayers. I rebuke and bind all the controlling forces of darkness standing against my prayers.

I declare that all satanic thrones, altars, dominions, principalities, powers, rulers of darkness, queens of the coast, queens of heavens, household wickedness, spiritual hosts of wickedness and all satanic works, have no power or authority over my life. I declare that satanic harassment and intimidation have no effect on me.

Today, I receive divine strength to pray; I will not pray in vain. I will not pray amiss. My prayers will bring the desired results. I command the fountain of prayer to open now, and to flow into my life, I command the warring angels of God to descend and fight on my behalf. Every minute and every hour that I spend in prayer, will bring solution. Every prayer point will attract divine attention and divine intervention. I decree open heavens over my prayers, and today, God of heaven and earth will attend to my case. My prayers today will shake the heavens and move the earth. Testimonies, miracles, healings, breakthroughs, and signs and wonders, will follow my prayers. At the end of this prayer session, my life will never be the same again.

PRAYER POINTS

1. O God my Father, thank you for being my God, my Father and my friend.
2. O God my Father, thank you for the privilege to know you and the power of the resurrection of Jesus Christ.
3. O God my Father, thank you for always being there for me and with me.
4. O God my Father, thank you for the great and mighty things that you are doing in my life.
5. O God my Father, thank you for your provision and protection over me and my household.
6. O God my Father, thank you for always answering my prayers.
7. I confess my sins before you today and I ask you to forgive me on the basis of your mercy, in the name of Jesus Christ.
8. Wash me clean today O Lord by the blood of Jesus Christ.
9. I cover myself and my household with the blood of Jesus Christ.
10. My prayers today will not go in vain; my prayers will produce the desired results in the name of Jesus Christ.
11. Representatives of hell that will not let me have peace at work, O God my Father, let the whirlwind of God violently blow them away, in the name of Jesus Christ.

12. Representatives of hell that will not let me have peace at home, O God my Father, let the whirlwind of God violently blow them away, in the name of Jesus Christ.

13. Representatives of hell that will not let me have peace in my neighborhood, O God my Father, let the whirlwind of God violently blow them away, in the name of Jesus Christ.

14. Representatives of hell that will not let me have peace in my family, O God my Father, let the whirlwind of God violently blow them away, in the name of Jesus Christ.

15. Representatives of hell that will not let me have peace among my friends, O God my Father, let the whirlwind of God violently blow them away, in the name of Jesus Christ.

16. Satanic contractors sent to rob me of my God given blessings, O God my Father, let the whirlwind of God violently blow them away, in the name of Jesus Christ.

17. Satanic contractors sent to monitor my outgoing and incoming, O God my Father, let the whirlwind of God violently blow them away, in the name of Jesus Christ.

18. Satanic contractors sent to cause confusion in my marriage, O God my Father, let the whirlwind of God violently blow them away, in the name of Jesus Christ.

19. Satanic contractors sent to make my life miserable, O God my Father, let the whirlwind of God violently blow them away, in the name of Jesus Christ.

20. Satanic contractors sent to make success impossible for me, O God my Father, let the whirlwind of God violently blow them away, in the name of Jesus Christ.

21. Satanic contractors sent to make breakthroughs impossible for me, O God my Father, let the whirlwind

of God violently blow them away, in the name of Jesus Christ.

22. Satanic contractors sent to infect me with sickness, O God my Father, let the whirlwind of God violently blow them away, in the name of Jesus Christ.

23. Satanic contractors sent to make it impossible for me to move forward in life, O God my Father, let the whirlwind of God violently blow them away, in the name of Jesus Christ.

24. Satanic contractors sent to pollute my prayer altar, O God my Father, let the whirlwind of God violently blow them away, in the name of Jesus Christ.

25. Satanic contractors sent to prolong my problems, O God my Father, let the whirlwind of God violently blow them away, in the name of Jesus Christ.

26. Satanic contractors sent to add affliction to afflictions in my life, O God my Father, let the whirlwind of God violently blow them away, in the name of Jesus Christ.

27. Satanic contractors sent to keep me in bondage, O God my Father, let the whirlwind of God violently blow them away, in the name of Jesus Christ.

28. Satanic contractors acting as my friends in order to get close to me, O God my Father, expose them and let the whirlwind of God violently blow them away, in the name of Jesus Christ.

29. Satanic contractors sent to hinder my prayers, enough is enough. O Lord, let the whirlwind of God violently blow them away, in the name of Jesus Christ.

30. Satanic contractors sent to corrupt my anointing, O God my Father, let the whirlwind violently blow them away, in the name of Jesus Christ.

31. Satanic contractors sent to keep me stagnated, enough is enough. O Lord, let the whirlwind of God violently blow them away, in the name of Jesus Christ.
32. Satanic contractors sent to abort my pregnancy of good things, O God my Father, let the whirlwind of God violently blow them away, in the name of Jesus Christ.
33. Satanic contractors sent to drive my helpers away from me, enough is enough. O Lord, let the whirlwind of God violently blow them away, in the name of Jesus Christ.
34. Satanic contractors sent to renew my solved problems, O God my Father this is not allowed, let the whirlwind of God violently blow them away, in the name of Jesus Christ.
35. Satanic contractors sent to kill me before my time, I will not die but live. O God my Father, let the whirlwind of God violently blow them away, in the name of Jesus Christ.

I cover my prayers in the blood of Jesus Christ. According to the Word of God, I have asked; I shall receive. I have knocked the door; it shall be opened unto me. I have sought; I shall find, in the name of Jesus Christ. It is written, "... Decree a thing, and it shall be established". As I have spoken in prayer, it shall be so. My prayers shall produce desired results. My prayers shall produce desired miracles. My prayers shall produce desired testimonies, in the name of Jesus Christ. Territorial spirit and power cannot hinder this prayer. Sins and flesh cannot hinder this prayer. It is done. It is sealed by the blood of Jesus Christ. It is delivered to me, in Jesus mighty name. Amen!

DAY EIGHT

THOU SHALT NOT TROUBLE ME

Passages To Read Before You Pray:
Job 5:12-13, Galatians 6:17, Zechariah 4:7,
Matthew 17:20, Psalms 18, 3, 86

In the book of Job 22:28, the Scripture says when I decree a thing, it shall be established for me. I stand on this Scripture and decree. I have come into the presence of God today to plead my case. I enter through the gate of praise into the sanctuary of heaven. I cover myself in the precious blood of Jesus Christ. I baptize myself in the fire of the Holy Ghost. I charge this atmosphere with the fire of God, and I take this neighborhood for the Lord. I arrest every principality and power, territorial spirit, and every throne and kingdom that is not of God. I cast you down and I command you never to lift yourself up against me, because I have the life of God in me.

In the name of Jesus Christ, I confess my sins today, and I ask you O Lord to forgive me on the basis of your mercy. With all my heart, I forgive those who have sinned against me from the past through this moment. I release them from any form of guilt and shame, in the name of Jesus Christ. I hereby plead the blood of Jesus over any sins committed by my parents and ancestors. I cancel through the Blood of Jesus Christ, any satanic covenants, exchanges, vows or transactions made over my life, body, soul, spirit, and circumstances, in the name of Jesus Christ. I cancel every legal right that the devil may have against me, by the blood of Jesus Christ. The accuser of the brethren will have nothing against me as I come to the presence of God in prayer.

The devil cannot hinder or delay my prayer, because I know who I am. I am a child of the Kingdom; I am a king and priest of the Lord, redeemed from the hand of the devil by the blood of Jesus Christ. I declare that all satanic thrones, altars, dominions, principalities, powers, rulers of darkness, queen of the coast, queen of heavens, household wickedness, spiritual hosts of wickedness and all satanic works, have no power or authority over my life. I declare that satanic harassment and intimidation have no effect on me.

Today I receive divine strength to pray; I will not pray in vain. I will not pray amiss. My prayers will bring the desired results. I command the fountain of prayer to open now, and flow into my life, I command the warring angels of God to descend and fight on my behalf. Every minute and every hour that I spend in prayer will bring solution. Every prayer point will attract divine attention and divine intervention. I decree open heavens over my prayers, and today, God of heaven and earth will attend to my case. My prayers today will shake the heavens and move the earth; testimonies, miracles, healing, breakthrough, signs and wonders will follow my prayers. At the end of this prayer session, my life will never be the same again.

PRAYER POINTS

1. O God my Father, thank you for being my God, my Father and my friend.
2. O God my Father, thank you for the privilege to know you and the power of the resurrection of Jesus Christ.
3. O God my Father, thank you for always being there for me and with me.

4. O God my Father, thank you for the great and mighty things that you are doing in my life.
5. O God my Father, thank you for your provision and protection over me and my household.
6. O God my Father, thank you for always answering my prayers.
7. I confess my sins before you today and I ask you to forgive me on the basis of your mercy, in the name of Jesus Christ.
8. Wash me clean today O Lord by the blood of Jesus Christ.
9. I cover myself and my household with the blood of Jesus Christ.
10. My prayers today will not go in vain; my prayers will produce the desired results in the name of Jesus Christ.
11. I destroy anything in my life giving my enemies access to do whatever they want in my life, in the name of Jesus Christ.
12. O God my Father, arise and perform your wonders in my life today, in the name of Jesus Christ.
13. Lord, I need a miracle. I cannot continue like this, in the name of Jesus Christ.
14. I stand on the Word of God and I take my life back today from the hands of the wicked, in the name of Jesus Christ.
15. By the authority in the blood of Jesus Christ, I repossess everything that the enemy has stolen from me, in the name of Jesus Christ.
16. By the authority in the blood of Jesus Christ, I withdraw the control of my life from the hands of household enemies, in the name of Jesus Christ.

17. By the power in the blood of Jesus Christ, I withdraw the control of my life from the hands and dominations of the powers of darkness, in the name of Jesus Christ.
18. O God my Father, let every negative energy around me be neutralized by the blood of Jesus Christ.
19. God has not created me for nothing. Today, I receive the anointing to walk into my purpose, in the name of Jesus Christ.
20. I will live to fulfill destiny, in the name of Jesus Christ.
21. O God my Father, arise and break by your fire, every satanic chain holding me captive, in the name of Jesus Christ.
22. O God my Father, arise and frustrate the plans of the wicked concerning my life, in the name of Jesus Christ.
23. I decree today that every demonic experiment against my life will not prosper, in the name of Jesus Christ.
24. O God my Father, let the activities of the enemy in my life come to a quick end, in the name of Jesus Christ.
25. By the power in the blood of Jesus, I arrest every demonic power attacking me because of my prayers, in the name of Jesus Christ.
26. By the power in the blood of Jesus, I paralyze every demonic power attacking me because of what God is doing in my life, in the name of Jesus Christ.
27. O God my Father, let your angels search the land of the dead and the living and restore all my stolen glory, in the name of Jesus Christ.
28. O God my Father, let your angels search the land of the dead and the living and restore all my stolen blessings, in the name of Jesus Christ.

29. O God my Father, let your angels search the land of the dead and the living and restore all my stolen virtues, in the name of Jesus Christ.
30. O God my Father, let your angels search the land of the dead and the living and restore all my stolen potentials, in the name of Jesus Christ.
31. O God my Father, arise and visit all evil shrines built against my family with thunder and earthquake, in the name of Jesus Christ.
32. O God my Father, arise and visit all evil altars built against my life with thunder and earthquake, in the name of Jesus Christ.
33. O God my Father, arise and visit all evil altars built against my family with thunder and earthquake, in the name of Jesus Christ.
34. O God my Father, arise and visit all evil temples built against my life with thunder and earthquake, in the name of Jesus Christ.
35. O God my Father, arise and visit all evil temples built against my family with thunder and earthquake, in the name of Jesus Christ.
36. I release the fire of God today, to destroy anything representing me on the evil altar, in the name of Jesus Christ.
37. I release the fire of God today, to destroy anything representing me in the kingdom of darkness, in the name of Jesus Christ.
38. Any problem challenging the power of God in my life, receive an immediate and permanent solution now, in the name of Jesus Christ.

39. By the power that set Israelites free from Egyptian bondage, God Almighty, set me free today from my stubborn situations, in the name of Jesus Christ.

40. Who are you? O Great Mountain of problem, you have no place in my life. I command you be removed and perish in the Red Sea, in the name of Jesus Christ.

41. Who are you? O Great Mountain of infirmity, you have no place in my life. I command you be removed and perish in the Red Sea, in the name of Jesus Christ.

42. Who are you? O Great Mountain of poverty, you have no place in my life. I command you be removed and perish in the Red Sea, in the name of Jesus Christ.

43. Who are you? O Great Mountain of frustration, you have no place in my life. I command you be removed and perish in the Red Sea, in the name of Jesus Christ.

44. Who are you? O Great Mountain of loneliness, you have no place in my life. I command you be removed and perish in the Red Sea, in the name of Jesus Christ.

45. Who are you? O Great Mountain of discouragement, you have no place in my life. I command you be removed and perish in the Red Sea, in the name of Jesus Christ.

46. Who are you? O Great Mountain of disappointment, you have no place in my life. I command you be removed and perish in the Red Sea, in the name of Jesus Christ.

47. In your name of Lord, there is power. Today, I receive the power to overcome every attack of the enemy, in the name of Jesus Christ.

48. In your name O Lord, there is deliverance. Today, I receive total deliverance from any form of captivity, in the name of Jesus Christ.

49. In your name O Lord, there is healing. Today, I receive total healing from any form of sickness and infirmity, in the name of Jesus Christ.

50. In your name O Lord, there is solution. Today, I receive solution to every challenge confronting me and my family, in the name of Jesus Christ.

51. O God my Father, let the owners of evil load in my life carry their load, in the name of Jesus Christ.

52. You power of death and hell, loose your hold over my life now, in the name of Jesus Christ.

53. You power of the grave, loose your hold over my life now, in the name of Jesus Christ.

54. Any power anywhere, prolonging my day of joy, you will not prosper; loose your hold over my life now, in the name of Jesus Christ.

55. O ye serpentine spirit, thou shalt not trouble me because I have the mark of Jesus Christ in my body, in the name of Jesus Christ.

56. O ye prince of Persia, thou shalt not trouble me because I have the mark of Jesus Christ in my body, in the name of Jesus Christ.

57. O ye territorial spirit, thou shalt not trouble me because I have the mark of Jesus Christ in my body, in the name of Jesus Christ.

58. O ye spirit of witchcraft, thou shalt not trouble me because I have the mark of Jesus Christ in my body, in the name of Jesus Christ.

59. O ye Jezebel spirit, thou shalt not trouble me because I have the mark of Jesus Christ in my body, in the name of Jesus Christ.

60. O ye queen of heaven, thou shalt not trouble me because I have the mark of Jesus Christ in my body, in the name of Jesus Christ.

61. O ye principalities and powers, thou shalt not trouble me because I have the mark of Jesus Christ in my body, in the name of Jesus Christ.

62. O ye spiritual wickedness in high places, thou shalt not trouble me because I have the mark of Jesus Christ in my body, in the name of Jesus Christ.

63. O ye rulers of darkness of this world, thou shalt not trouble me because I have the mark of Jesus Christ in my body, in the name of Jesus Christ.

64. O ye water spirit, thou shalt not trouble me because I have the mark of Jesus Christ in my body, in the name of Jesus Christ.

65. O ye household enemies, thou shalt not trouble me because I have the mark of Jesus Christ in my body, in the name of Jesus Christ.

66. O ye power of the night, thou shalt not trouble me because I have the mark of Jesus Christ in my body, in the name of Jesus Christ.

67. O God my Father, let the blood of Jesus Christ erase evil identification mark in every area of my life, in the name of Jesus Christ.

68. My body is the temple of the Holy Ghost. I have the fire of God in me; let every work of the devil in my body be consumed by the fire of God, in the name of Jesus Christ.

69. My body is the temple of the Holy Ghost. I have the fire of God in me; let every sickness in my body be consumed by the fire of God, in the name of Jesus Christ.

70. My body is the temple of the Holy Ghost. I have the fire of God in me; let every mark of hatred in my body be consumed by the fire of God, in the name of Jesus Christ.

71. My body is the temple of the Holy Ghost. I have the fire of God in me; let every arrow of the devil in my body be consumed by the fire of God, in the name of Jesus Christ.

72. My body is the temple of the Holy Ghost. I have the fire of God in me; let every evil deposit in my body be consumed by the fire of God, in the name of Jesus Christ.

73. My body is the temple of the Holy Ghost. I have the fire of God in me; let every evil seed sown into my body be consumed by the fire of God, in the name of Jesus Christ.

74. By the authority of the Word of God, I command my overdue blessings to be released unto me now, in the name of Jesus Christ.

75. By the authority of the Word of God, I command my overdue miracles to be released unto me now, in the name of Jesus Christ.

76. By the authority of the Word of God, I command my overdue promotion to be released unto me now, in the name of Jesus Christ.

77. By the authority of the Word of God, I command my overdue breakthroughs to be released unto me now, in the name of Jesus Christ.

78. By the authority of the Word of God, I command my overdue increase to be released unto me now, in the name of Jesus Christ.

79. It is written, angels of God will encompass me round about because I fear the Lord, in the name of Jesus Christ.

80. It is written, the angels of God will carry me and my family in their hands so that we will never hit our feet against a stone, in the name of Jesus Christ.

I cover my prayers in the blood of Jesus Christ. According to the Word of God, I have asked, I shall receive. I have knocked the door, it shall be opened unto me. I have sought, I shall find, in the name of Jesus Christ. It is written, "… Decree a thing, and it shall be established". As I have spoken in prayer, it shall be so. My prayers shall produce desire results. My prayers shall produce desired miracles. My prayers shall produce desired testimonies, in the name of Jesus Christ. Territorial spirit and power cannot hinder this prayer. Sins and flesh cannot hinder this prayer. It is done. It is sealed by the blood of Jesus Christ. It is delivered to me, in Jesus might name. Amen!

DAY NINE

PRAYER TO TAKE YOUR LIFE BACK

Passages To Read Before You Pray:
Matthew 11:12, Psalms 3, 9, 18, 35, 68, 70, 109

In the book of Job 22:28, the Scripture says when I decree a thing, it shall be established for me. I stand on this Scripture and decree. I have come today to fellowship with my heavenly Father, and make my requests and needs known unto Him. I cannot be hindered nor delayed because I know who I am in the Lord. I am a child of the Kingdom, born of the Spirit, redeemed by the blood of Jesus Christ. I walk in authority, living life without any apology because the power and authority has been given to me according to the Word of God in the book of Luke 9:1.

As I have come to pray today and to fellowship with my heavenly Father, I cover myself in the blood of Jesus Christ, and I put on the whole armor of God. I hereby come against every Prince of Persia that wants to hinder my prayer, I arrest you by the power in the blood of Jesus Christ, and I bind you and cast you down into the pit of hell.

I come against principalities and powers that wrestle with me and my prayers, I arrest you today by the power in the name of Jesus Christ, and I bind you and cast down into the pit of hell. I come against the rulers of the darkness of this world, against spiritual wickedness in high places, I arrest you all by the power in the name of Jesus Christ, and I bind you and cast you down into the pit of hell. I come against weakness and weariness, I arrest you today by the power in the name of Jesus Christ, and I bind you and cast you out of my life. I come against wondering

90

spirit and distractions, I arrest you today by the power in the name of Jesus Christ, and I bind you and cast you out of my life.

Today I receive the anointing to pray and get results, my prayers cannot be hindered nor delayed because Jesus is my Lord, I will pray today and get the desired results, I decree open heavens upon my prayers. I baptize myself in the fire of the Holy Ghost; therefore I have become too hot for the enemy to handle. My prayers today will attract divine intervention to every situation in my life; signs and wonders will follow my prayers today, testimonies will follow my prayers today and the name of God alone will be glorified, in Jesus name. Amen!

PRAYER POINTS

1. O God my Father, thank you for being my God, my Father and my friend.
2. O God my Father, thank you for the privilege to know you and the power of the resurrection of Jesus Christ.
3. O God my Father, thank you for always being there for me and with me.
4. O God my Father, thank you for the great and mighty things that you are doing in my life.
5. O God my Father, thank you for your provision and protection over me and my household.
6. O God my Father, thank you for always answering my prayers.
7. I confess my sins before you today and I ask you to forgive me on the basis of your mercy, in the name of Jesus Christ.

8. Wash me clean today O Lord by the blood of Jesus Christ.

9. I cover myself and my household with the blood of Jesus Christ.

10. My prayers today will not go in vain; my prayers will produce the desired results in the name of Jesus Christ.

11. Today O Lord, I take my life back by force, from the hands of every power that wants to keep me in bondage.

12. Today O Lord, I take my life back from the hands of the household wickedness.

13. Today O Lord, I take my life back by force from the hands of the power of poverty.

14. Today O Lord, I take my life back by force from the hands of the power that wants me to die poor.

15. Today O Lord, I take my life back by force from the hands of the power that wants me to struggle and never make it.

16. Today O Lord, I take my life back by force from the hands of the power that wants me to die alone.

17. Today O Lord, I take my life back by force from the hands of the evil controller that is controlling my life.

18. Today O Lord, I take my life back by force from the hands of evil manipulators, manipulating me in any way.

19. Today O Lord, I take my life back by force from the hands of the power that's refueling my problems.

20. Today O Lord, I take my life back by force from the hands of the power that's turning my helpers against me.

21. Today O Lord, I take my life back by force from the hands of the power that wants to destroy my life.

22. Today O Lord, I take my life back by force from the hands of the power that wants to destroy my future.

23. Today O Lord, I take my life back by force from the hands of the Pharaoh terrorizing me day and night.
24. Today O Lord, I take my life back by force from the hands of the power that wants to make my life a living hell.
25. Today O Lord, I take my life back by force from the hands of the power that vows that I will never make it in life no matter how much I try.
26. Today O Lord, I take my life back by force from the bondage of fear.
27. Today O Lord, I take my life back by force from the fear of failure.
28. All the blessings stolen away from me, I take it back by force.
29. My breakthroughs that have been taken away from me, today I take it back by force.
30. My miracle that has been hindered by the enemy, today I take it back by force.
31. Promotion that has been eluding me all this time, today I take it by force.
32. Financial prosperity that I have been waiting for me but I am yet to receive, today I take it by force.
33. Open heavens that I have been expecting to manifest in my life but have yet to happen, I take it by force.
34. Business opportunities that I have been praying for but have yet to manifest, today I take it by force.
35. O God my Father, I have been praying for a long time for victory over the attack of the enemy, today I take it by force.
36. The good job and stable employment that I have been praying for which has yet to manifest, today O Lord, I take it by force.

37. The nice house that I have been praying for which is yet to manifest, today I take it by force.
38. Success in every area that I have been praying for but is yet to manifest, today O Lord, I take it by force.
39. My blessing that has fallen into wrong hands, today I take it back by force.
40. My promotion that has been given to another person, today I take it back by force.
41. My miracles that have been hindered by the enemy, today I take it back by force.
42. Answers to my prayers that have been delayed by the Prince of Persia, today I take it back by force.
43. My breakthroughs that have fallen into wrong hands, today I take it back by force.
44. Good things that I have lost because of ignorance, today I take it back by force.
45. Good things that I have lost because of sin, I repent today and I take it back by force.
46. The promise of God for me that is yet to be fulfilled, today I take it by force.
47. Good things that the enemy says can never happen in my life, today O Lord, it take it by force.
48. The breakthrough that everyone around me believes I can never achieve in life, today O Lord, I take it by force.
49. The position that everyone around me believes I can never get it in life, today O Lord, I take it by force.
50. The situation that everyone around me believes I can never overcome, today O Lord, I overcome this situation by force.

51. The pit of hopelessness that everyone around me believes I can never get out of, today O Lord, I am getting out by force.

52. The wilderness of trouble that everyone around me believes I can never get out of, today O Lord, I am getting out by force.

53. The stubborn situation that everyone around me believes I can never overcome, today O Lord, I overcome this situation by force.

54. Today O Lord, I take my life back by force from the hands of the power that wants to kill my dreams.

55. Today O Lord, I take my life back by force from the hands of the power that wants to destroy my destiny.

56. Today O Lord, I take my life back from the hands of the power that is using my life for an experiment.

57. Today O Lord, I take my life back by force from the hands of the power of darkness that is using my life to get promotion.

58. Today O Lord, I take my life back by force from the hands of the power that is prolonging my journey to my promise land.

59. Today O Lord, I take my life back by force from the foundational curse affecting my bloodline.

60. Today O Lord, I take my life back by force from the generational curse affecting my bloodline.

61. Today O Lord, I take my life back by force from the curse of failure that is affecting my progress in life.

62. Today O Lord, I take my life back by force from the curse of failure that is affecting my desired success.

63. Today O Lord, I take my life back by force from the curse of poverty that is affecting the works of my hands.

64. Today O Lord, I take my life back by force from the curse of poverty that is destroying my harvest.
65. Today O Lord, I take my life back by force from the hands of the power assigned to increase my pain.
66. Today O Lord, I take my life back by force from the hands of the power assigned to make my life miserable.
67. Today O Lord, I take my life back by force from the hands of the power assigned to make success impossible for me.
68. Today O Lord, I take my life back by force from the hands of the power assigned to make it impossible for me to breakthrough in life.
69. Today O Lord, I take my life back by force from the hands of the power assigned to frustrate me.
70. Today O Lord, I take my life back by force from the hands of the wicked. Let the wickedness of the wicked fall upon their own heads.

I cover my prayers in the blood of Jesus Christ. According to the Word of God, I have asked; I shall receive. I have knocked the door; it shall be opened unto me. I have sought; I shall find, in the name of Jesus Christ. It is written, "... Decree a thing, and it shall be established". As I have spoken in prayer, it shall be so. My prayers shall produce desired results. My prayers shall produce desired miracles. My prayers shall produce desired testimonies, in the name of Jesus Christ. Territorial spirit and power cannot hinder this prayer. Sins and flesh cannot hinder this prayer. It is done. It is sealed by the blood of Jesus Christ. It is delivered to me, in Jesus mighty name. Amen!

DAY TEN

OVERCOMING JEZEBEL SPIRIT

Passages To Read Before You Pray:
Revelation 2:20, 1 Kings 18:4, 13, 1 Kings 19:1-2,
2 Kings 9:20-37, Psalms 109

In the book of Job 22:28, the Scripture says when I decree a thing, it shall be established for me. I stand on this Scripture and decree. I have come into the presence of God today to plead my case. I enter through the gate of praise into the sanctuary of heaven. I cover myself in the precious blood of Jesus Christ. I baptize myself in the fire of the Holy Ghost. I charge this atmosphere with the fire of God, and I take this neighborhood for the Lord. I arrest every principality and power, territorial spirit, and every throne and kingdom that is not of God. I cast you down and I command you never to lift yourself up against me, because I have the life of God in me.

In the name of Jesus Christ, I confess my sins today, and I ask you O Lord to forgive me on the basis of your mercy. With all my heart, I forgive those who have sinned against me from the past through this moment. I release them from any form of guilt and shame, in the name of Jesus Christ. I hereby plead the blood of Jesus over any sins committed by my parents and ancestors. I cancel through the Blood of Jesus Christ, any satanic covenants, exchanges, vows or transactions made over my life, body, soul, spirit, and circumstances, in the name of Jesus Christ. I cancel every legal right that the devil may have against me, by the blood of Jesus Christ. The accuser of the brethren will have nothing against me as I come to the presence of God in prayer.

The devil cannot hinder or delay my prayer, because I know who I am. I am a child of the Kingdom; I am a king and priest of the Lord, redeemed from the hand of the devil by the blood of Jesus Christ. I declare that all satanic thrones, altars, dominions, principalities, powers, rulers of darkness, queen of the coast, queen of heavens, household wickedness, spiritual hosts of wickedness and all satanic works, have no power or authority over my life. I declare that satanic harassment and intimidation have no effect on me.

Today I receive divine strength to pray; I will not pray in vain. I will not pray amiss. My prayers will bring the desired results. I command the fountain of prayer to open now, and flow into my life, I command the warring angels of God to descend and fight on my behalf. Every minute and every hour that I spend in prayer will bring solution. Every prayer point will attract divine attention and divine intervention. I decree open heavens over my prayers, and today, God of heaven and earth will attend to my case. My prayers today will shake the heavens and move the earth; testimonies, miracles, healing, breakthrough, signs and wonders will follow my prayers. At the end of this prayer session, my life will never be the same again.

PRAYER POINTS

1. O God my Father, thank you for being my God, my Father and my friend.
2. O God my Father, thank you for the privilege to know you and the power of the resurrection of Jesus Christ.
3. O God my Father, thank you for always being there for me and with me.

4. O God my Father, thank you for the great and mighty things that you are doing in my life.
5. O God my Father, thank you for your provision and protection over me and my household.
6. O God my Father, thank you for always answering my prayers.
7. I confess my sins before you today and I ask you to forgive me on the basis of your mercy, in the name of Jesus Christ.
8. Wash me clean today O Lord by the blood of Jesus Christ.
9. I cover myself and my household with the blood of Jesus Christ.
10. My prayers today will not go in vain; my prayers will produce the desired results in the name of Jesus Christ.
11. I cover myself and my household in the blood of Jesus Christ.
12. I cover everything concerning me in the blood of Jesus Christ.
13. I put on the whole armor of God and I stand against the wiles of the devil.
14. By the authority in the name of Jesus Christ, I challenge every Jezebel spirit working against me.
15. By the authority in the name of Jesus Christ, I arrest every Jezebel spirit working against me.
16. O God my Father, let every Jezebel spirit working against me be exposed and put to an open shame.
17. By the power in the name of Jesus Christ, I put an end to every wicked attack launched against me by Jezebel spirit.

18. By the power in the name of Jesus Christ, I put an end to every wicked attack launched against my family by Jezebel spirit.

19. By the power in the name of Jesus Christ, I put an end to every wicked attack launched against my marriage by Jezebel spirit.

20. By the power in the name of Jesus Christ, I put an end to every wicked attack launched against my finances by Jezebel spirit.

21. By the power in the name of Jesus Christ, I put an end to every wicked attack launched against my ministry by Jezebel spirit.

22. By the power in the name of Jesus Christ, I put an end to every wicked attack launched against my progress by Jezebel spirit.

23. By the power in the name of Jesus Christ, I put an end to every wicked attack launched against my children by Jezebel spirit.

24. Today, I receive victory over Jezebel spirit that is working against me.

25. Every crafty spirit of Jezebel around me, be exposed and be rendered useless, in the name of Jesus Christ.

26. Every crafty spirit of Jezebel around me will not prosper, in the name of Jesus Christ.

27. O God my Father, let dangerous messengers of Jezebel spirit working against me be frustrated.

28. O God my Father, let dangerous messengers of Jezebel spirit working against me be disappointed.

29. O God my Father, let dangerous messengers of Jezebel spirit working against me receive double destruction.

30. I command the dedicated students of Jezebel spirit assigned against me to be confused and frustrated, in the name of Jesus Christ.

31. I command the dedicated students of Jezebel spirit assigned against my marriage to receive sudden destruction.

32. I command the dedicated students of Jezebel spirit assigned to frustrate me to receive sudden destruction.

33. I command the dedicated students of Jezebel spirit assigned to monitor my life to receive double destruction.

34. I command the dedicated students of Jezebel spirit assigned to control my life to receive double destruction.

35. I command the dedicated students of Jezebel spirit assigned to infiltrate my ministry to receive sudden destruction.

36. I command the dedicated students of Jezebel spirit assigned to destroy my marriage to receive double destruction.

37. I command the dedicated students of Jezebel spirit assigned to manipulate my spouse to receive double destruction.

38. I command the dedicated students of Jezebel spirit assigned to manipulate me to receive sudden destruction.

39. Today, I neutralize every plan of Jezebel spirit to make my life miserable, in the name of Jesus Christ.

40. Today, I destroy every work of Jezebel spirit to make my life miserable, in the name of Jesus Christ.

41. Today, I cancel every activity of Jezebel spirit to make my life miserable, in the name of Jesus Christ.

42. Every controlling spirit working tirelessly to control my mind, I arrest you and cast you out of my mind, in the name of Jesus Christ.

43. Spirit of witchcraft working tirelessly to control my life, I bind and cast you out of my life, in the name of Jesus Christ.

44. Every unseen spirit trying to destroy my life, be destroyed by the fire of God.

45. Every unseen spirit trying to destroy my marriage, be destroyed by the fire of God.

46. Every unseen spirit trying to destroy my family, be destroyed by the fire of God.

47. Every unseen spirit trying to destroy my ministry, be destroyed by the fire of God.

48. Every unseen spirit trying to destroy my future, be destroyed by the fire of God.

49. Any form of control used against me by Jezebel spirit will not prosper.

50. I receive the anointing to see through Jezebel's deceitful camouflage.

51. I break every chain of Jezebel spirit in my life, in the name of Jesus Christ.

52. Today I am delivered from Jezebel spirit that is using me without my knowledge.

53. Today I am delivered from Jezebel spirit that is using me against myself.

54. Today I am delivered from Jezebel spirit that is using me to destroy my own peace.

55. Today I am delivered from Jezebel spirit that is using me to destroy my own home.

56. Today I am delivered from Jezebel spirit that is turning my spouse against me.

57. Today I am delivered from Jezebel spirit that is turning my children against me.
58. Today I break free from the bondage of Jezebel spirit, in the name of Jesus Christ.
59. Jesus Christ is Lord over my life. Jezebel spirit cannot rule over me.
60. Jesus Christ is Lord over my life. Jezebel cannot control me.

I cover my prayers in the blood of Jesus Christ. According to the Word of God, I have asked, I shall receive. I have knocked the door, it shall be opened unto me. I have sought, I shall find, in the name of Jesus Christ. It is written, "… Decree a thing, and it shall be established". As I have spoken in prayer, it shall be so. My prayers shall produce desire results. My prayers shall produce desired miracles. My prayers shall produce desired testimonies, in the name of Jesus Christ. Territorial spirit and power cannot hinder this prayer. Sins and flesh cannot hinder this prayer. It is done. It is sealed by the blood of Jesus Christ. It is delivered to me, in Jesus might name. Amen!

DAY ELEVEN

PRAYER TO CREATE A NO-FLY ZONE

Passages To Read Before You Pray:

1 Samuel 19:9-24, Psalms 23, 91, 34, 17, 68, 35, 109

In the book of Job 22:28, the Scripture says when I decree a thing, it shall be established for me. I stand on this Scripture and decree. I have come into the presence of God today to plead my case. I enter through the gate of praise, into the sanctuary of heaven. I cover myself in the precious blood of Jesus Christ. I baptize myself in the fire of the Holy Ghost. I charge this atmosphere with the fire of God, and I take this neighborhood for the Lord. I arrest every principality and power, territorial spirit, and every throne and kingdom that is not of God. I cast you down and I command you never to lift yourself up against me, because I have the life of God in me.

In the name of Jesus Christ, I confess my sins today, and I ask you O Lord to forgive me on the basis of your mercy. With all my heart, I forgive those who have sinned against me; from the past through this moment. I release them from any form of guilt and shame, in the name of Jesus Christ. I hereby plead the blood of Jesus over any sins committed by my parents and ancestors. I cancel through the Blood of Jesus Christ, any satanic covenants, exchanges, vows or transactions, made over my life, body, soul, spirit, and circumstances, in the name of Jesus Christ. I cancel every legal right that the devil may have against me, by the blood of Jesus Christ. The accuser of the brethren will have nothing against me, as I come to the presence of God in prayer.

The devil cannot hinder or delay my prayer, because I know who I am. I am a child of the Kingdom. I am a king and priest of the

106

Lord, redeemed from the hand of the devil by the blood of Jesus Christ. I walk in power. I walk in miracle. Proverbs 18:21 says, death and life are in the power of my tongue; I command the power in my tongue to manifest now. I command my tongue to become fire, to consume all the powers of darkness in the air, the land, the sea, and beneath the earth. I hereby raise Holy Ghost standard against the prince of the power of the air and all the hosts of darkness in the air. I raise Holy Ghost standard against the queen of the coasts and all the hosts of darkness on the land. I raise Holy Ghost standard against the marine kingdom and all the hosts of darkness in the sea. I raise Holy Ghost standard against the kingdom of hell and all the hosts of darkness beneath the earth. I shoot down all the networks of demons gathering to resist my prayers. I rebuke and bind all the controlling forces of darkness standing against my prayers.

I declare that all satanic thrones, altars, dominions, principalities, powers, rulers of darkness, queens of the coast, queens of heavens, household wickedness, spiritual hosts of wickedness and all satanic works, have no power or authority over my life. I declare that satanic harassment and intimidation have no effect on me.

Today, I receive divine strength to pray; I will not pray in vain. I will not pray amiss. My prayers will bring the desired results. I command the fountain of prayer to open now, and to flow into my life, I command the warring angels of God to descend and fight on my behalf. Every minute and every hour that I spend in prayer, will bring solution. Every prayer point will attract divine attention and divine intervention. I decree open heavens over my prayers, and today, God of heaven and earth will attend to my case. My prayers today will shake the heavens and move the earth. Testimonies, miracles, healings, breakthroughs, and signs and wonders, will follow my prayers. At the end of this prayer session, my life will never be the same again.

PRAYER POINTS

1. O God my Father, thank you for being my God, my Father and my friend.
2. O God my Father, thank you for the privilege to know you and the power of the resurrection of Jesus Christ.
3. O God my Father, thank you for always being there for me and with me.
4. O God my Father, thank you for the great and mighty things that you are doing in my life.
5. O God my Father, thank you for your provision and protection over me and my household.
6. O God my Father, thank you for always answering my prayers.
7. I confess my sins before you today and I ask you to forgive me on the basis of your mercy, in the name of Jesus Christ.
8. Wash me clean today O Lord by the blood of Jesus Christ.
9. I cover myself and my household with the blood of Jesus Christ.
10. My prayers today will not go in vain; my prayers will produce the desired results in the name of Jesus Christ.
11. I stand on the Word of God; I create a no-fly zone around myself, an area over which the enemies are not permitted to operate, in the name of Jesus Christ.

12. I stand on the Word of God; I create a no-fly zone around my family, an area over which the enemies are not permitted to operate, in the name of Jesus Christ.

13. I stand on the Word of God; I create a no-fly zone around my marriage, an area over which the enemies are not permitted to operate, in the name of Jesus Christ.

14. I stand on the Word of God; I create a no-fly zone around my spouse, an area over which the enemies are not permitted to operate, in the name of Jesus Christ.

15. I stand on the Word of God; I create a no-fly zone around my children, an area over which the enemies are not permitted to operate, in the name of Jesus Christ.

16. I stand on the Word of God; I create a no-fly zone around my home, an area over which the enemies are not permitted to operate, in the name of Jesus Christ.

17. I stand on the Word of God; I create a no-fly zone around my business, an area over which the enemies are not permitted to operate, in the name of Jesus Christ.

18. I stand on the Word of God; I create a no-fly zone around my ministry, an area over which the enemies are not permitted to operate, in the name of Jesus Christ.

19. I stand on the Word of God; I create a no-fly zone around my finances, an area over which the enemies are not permitted to operate, in the name of Jesus Christ.

20. I draw the bloodline around myself which the enemy cannot cross, in the name of Jesus Christ.

21. I draw the bloodline around my family which the enemy cannot cross, in the name of Jesus Christ.

22. I draw the bloodline around my marriage which the enemy cannot cross, in the name of Jesus Christ.

23. I draw the bloodline around my ministry which the enemy cannot cross, in the name of Jesus Christ.

24. I build the edge of fire around my family; we are untouchable, in the name of Jesus Christ.
25. I build the edge of fire around my marriage; my marriage becomes untouchable, in the name of Jesus Christ.
26. I build the edge of fire around my children; my children become untouchable, in the name of Jesus Christ.
27. I build the edge of fire around my spouse; my spouse is untouchable, in the name of Jesus Christ.
28. I stand on the Word of God; I declare my home a no-fly zone for the enemy, in the name of Jesus Christ.
29. I stand on the Word of God; I declare my neighborhood a no-fly zone for the enemy, in the name of Jesus Christ.
30. I stand on the Word of God; I declare the city where I live a no-fly zone for the enemy, in the name of Jesus Christ.
31. I stand on the Word of God; I declare my air space a no-fly zone for the enemy, in the name of Jesus Christ.
32. O God my Father, send your angels to build walls of protection around me, in the name of Jesus Christ.
33. O God my Father, send your angels to build walls of protection around my home, in the name of Jesus Christ.
34. O God my Father, send your angels to build walls of protection around my family, in the name of Jesus Christ.
35. I stand on the Word of God; I decree and declare that satanic operation is prohibited in every area of my life, in the name of Jesus Christ.
36. I stand on the Word of God; I decree and declare that satanic operation is prohibited in my home, in the name of Jesus Christ.

37. I stand on the Word of God; I decree and declare that satanic operation is prohibited in my marriage, in the name of Jesus Christ.

38. I stand on the Word of God; I decree and declare that satanic operation against my spouse is prohibited, in the name of Jesus Christ.

39. I stand on the Word of God; I decree and declare that satanic operation against my children is prohibited, in the name of Jesus Christ.

40. I stand on the Word of God; I decree and declare that satanic operation against my family is prohibited, in the name of Jesus Christ.

41. I stand on the Word of God; I decree and declare that satanic operation against my destiny is prohibited, in the name of Jesus Christ.

42. I stand on the Word of God; I decree and declare that satanic operation against my future is prohibited, in the name of Jesus Christ.

43. I stand on the Word of God; I decree and declare that satanic operation against my finances is prohibited, in the name of Jesus Christ.

44. I stand on the Word of God; I decree and declare that satanic operation against my dreams is prohibited, in the name of Jesus Christ.

45. I stand on the Word of God; I decree and declare that satanic operation against my purpose is prohibited, in the name of Jesus Christ.

46. I stand on the Word of God; I decree and declare that satanic operation against my goals is prohibited, in the name of Jesus Christ.

47. I stand on the Word of God; I decree and declare that satanic operation against the works of my hands is prohibited, in the name of Jesus Christ.

48. I stand on the Word of God; I decree and declare that satanic operation against my ministry is prohibited, in the name of Jesus Christ.

49. I stand on the Word of God; I decree and declare that satanic operation against my spiritual life is prohibited, in the name of Jesus Christ.

50. I stand on the Word of God; I decree and declare that satanic operation against my spiritual growth is prohibited, in the name of Jesus Christ.

51. I stand on the Word of God; I decree and declare that satanic operation in my dreams is prohibited, in the name of Jesus Christ.

52. I stand on the Word of God; I command any power anywhere trying to break my no-fly zone to be shot down by the fire of God, in the name of Jesus Christ.

53. I stand on the Word of God; I command any power anywhere trying to attack me to be shot down by the fire of God, in the name of Jesus Christ.

54. I stand on the Word of God; I command any power anywhere trying to attack my spouse to be shot down by the fire of God, in the name of Jesus Christ.

55. I stand on the Word of God; I command any power anywhere trying to attack my children to be shot down by the fire of God, in the name of Jesus Christ.

56. I stand on the Word of God; I command any power anywhere trying to attack my marriage to be shot down by the fire of God, in the name of Jesus Christ.

57. I stand on the Word of God; I command any power anywhere trying to attack my peace to be shot down by the fire of God, in the name of Jesus Christ.

58. I stand on the Word of God; I command any power anywhere trying to attack my joy to be shot down by the fire of God, in the name of Jesus Christ.

59. I stand on the Word of God; I command any power anywhere trying to attack my finances to be shot down by the fire of God, in the name of Jesus Christ.

60. I stand on the Word of God; I command any power anywhere trying to attack my job to be shot down by the fire of God, in the name of Jesus Christ.

61. I stand on the Word of God; I command any power anywhere trying to attack my business to be shot down by the fire of God, in the name of Jesus Christ.

62. I stand on the Word of God; I command any power anywhere trying to attack my quiet enjoyment to be shot down by the fire of God, in the name of Jesus Christ.

63. By the authority in the name of Jesus Christ; I release air fire power to destroy any power anywhere attacking me from the kingdom of darkness in the air, in the name of Jesus Christ.

64. By the authority in the name of Jesus Christ; I release air fire power to destroy any power anywhere attacking me from the marine kingdom of darkness, in the name of Jesus Christ.

65. By the authority in the name of Jesus Christ; I release air fire power to destroy any power anywhere attacking me from the kingdom of darkness on the land, in the name of Jesus Christ.

66. By the authority in the name of Jesus Christ; I release air fire power to destroy any power anywhere attacking me

from the kingdom of darkness beneath the ground, in the name of Jesus Christ.

67. By the authority in the name of Jesus Christ; I release air fire power to destroy any power anywhere attacking me from the kingdom of hell, in the name of Jesus Christ.

68. I dispatch the warring angels of heaven to conduct hourly air control operation over my neighborhood, and shoot down any trespasser, in the name of Jesus Christ.

69. I dispatch the warring angels of heaven to conduct hourly air control operation over my home, and shoot down any trespasser, in the name of Jesus Christ.

70. I dispatch the warring angels of heaven to conduct hourly air control operation over my city, and shoot down any trespasser, in the name of Jesus Christ.

71. I dispatch the warring angels of heaven to conduct hourly air control operation over my territory, and shoot down any trespasser, in the name of Jesus Christ.

72. O God my Father; let heavenly precision-strike weapons be released to destroy every difficult-to-reach targets in the camp of my enemy, in the name of Jesus Christ.

73. O God my Father; let heavenly precision-strike weapons be released to destroy every difficult-to-reach targets in the kingdom of darkness that has been troubling my life, in the name of Jesus Christ.

74. O God my Father; let heavenly precision-strike weapons be released to destroy every difficult-to-reach targets in the kingdom of darkness that has been troubling my marriage, in the name of Jesus Christ.

75. O God my Father; let heavenly precision-strike weapons be released to destroy every difficult-to-reach targets in the kingdom of darkness that has been hindering my blessing, in the name of Jesus Christ.

76. O God my Father; let heavenly precision-strike weapons be released to destroy every difficult-to-reach targets in the kingdom of darkness that has been delaying my miracles, in the name of Jesus Christ.

77. O God my Father; let heavenly precision-strike weapons be released to destroy every difficult-to-reach targets in the kingdom of darkness that has been holding my life back, in the name of Jesus Christ.

78. O God my Father; let heavenly precision-strike weapons be released to destroy every difficult-to-reach targets in the kingdom of darkness that has been attacking my family, in the name of Jesus Christ.

79. O God my Father; let heavenly precision-strike weapons be released to destroy every difficult-to-reach targets in the camp of my household wickedness, in the name of Jesus Christ.

80. O God my Father; let heavenly precision-strike weapons be released to destroy every evil power of my father's house that is difficult to reach, in the name of Jesus Christ.

81. O God my Father; let heavenly precision-strike weapons be released to destroy every evil power of my mother's house that is difficult to reach, in the name of Jesus Christ.

82. O God my Father; let heavenly precision-strike weapons be released to destroy every evil power in my neighborhood that is difficult to reach, in the name of Jesus Christ.

83. O God my Father; let heavenly precision-strike weapons be released to destroy every evil power in my family that is difficult to reach, in the name of Jesus Christ.

84. Psalms 34:7 says, the angels of God encamp around those who fear Him, and deliver them. O God my Father; surround me with your angels, in the name of Jesus Christ.

85. Psalms 34:7 says, the angels of God encamp around those who fear Him, and deliver them. O God my Father; surround my family with your angels, in the name of Jesus Christ.

86. Psalms 34:7 says, the angels of God encamp around those who fear Him, and deliver them. O God my Father; surround my spouse with your angels, in the name of Jesus Christ.

87. Psalms 34:7 says, the angels of God encamp around those who fear Him, and deliver them. O God my Father; surround my children with your angels, in the name of Jesus Christ.

88. Psalms 34:7 says, the angels of God encamp around those who fear Him, and deliver them. O God my Father; surround my marriage with your angels, in the name of Jesus Christ.

89. Psalms 34:7 says, the angels of God encamp around those who fear Him, and deliver them. O God my Father; surround my entire household with your angels, in the name of Jesus Christ.

90. I soak myself in the precious blood of Jesus Christ. I am well protected and secured in the Lord, in the name of Jesus Christ.

I cover my prayers in the blood of Jesus Christ. According to the Word of God, I have asked; I shall receive. I have knocked the door; it shall be opened unto me. I have sought; I shall find, in the name of Jesus Christ. It is written, "… Decree a thing, and it shall be established". As I have spoken in prayer, it shall be so. My prayers shall produce desired results. My prayers shall produce desired miracles. My prayers shall produce desired testimonies, in the name of Jesus Christ. Territorial spirit and power cannot hinder this prayer. Sins and flesh cannot hinder this prayer. It is done. It is sealed by the blood of Jesus Christ. It is delivered to me, in Jesus mighty name. Amen!

DAY TWELVE

PRAYER TO SHUT THE DOOR
AGAINST THE DEVIL

Passages To Read Before You Pray:
Matthew 18:18, Isaiah 22:22, Matthew 16:19,
Isaiah 45:2-3

In the book of Job 22:28, the Scripture says when I decree a thing, it shall be established for me. I stand on this Scripture and decree. I have come into the presence of God today to plead my case. I enter through the gate of praise into the sanctuary of heaven. I cover myself in the precious blood of Jesus Christ. I baptize myself in the fire of the Holy Ghost. I charge this atmosphere with the fire of God, and I take this neighborhood for the Lord. I arrest every principality and power, territorial spirit, and every throne and kingdom that is not of God. I cast you down and I command you never to lift yourself up against me, because I have the life of God in me.

In the name of Jesus Christ, I confess my sins today, and I ask you O Lord to forgive me on the basis of your mercy. With all my heart, I forgive those who have sinned against me from the past through this moment. I release them from any form of guilt and shame, in the name of Jesus Christ. I hereby plead the blood of Jesus over any sins committed by my parents and ancestors. I cancel through the Blood of Jesus Christ, any satanic covenants, exchanges, vows or transactions made over my life, body, soul, spirit, and circumstances, in the name of Jesus Christ. I cancel every legal right that the devil may have against me, by the blood of Jesus Christ. The accuser of the brethren will have nothing against me as I come to the presence of God in prayer.

The devil cannot hinder or delay my prayer, because I know who I am. I am a child of the Kingdom; I am a king and priest of the Lord, redeemed from the hand of the devil by the blood of Jesus Christ. I declare that all satanic thrones, altars, dominions, principalities, powers, rulers of darkness, queen of the coast, queen of heavens, household wickedness, spiritual hosts of wickedness and all satanic works, have no power or authority over my life. I declare that satanic harassment and intimidation have no effect on me.

Today I receive divine strength to pray; I will not pray in vain. I will not pray amiss. My prayers will bring the desired results. I command the fountain of prayer to open now, and flow into my life, I command the warring angels of God to descend and fight on my behalf. Every minute and every hour that I spend in prayer will bring solution. Every prayer point will attract divine attention and divine intervention. I decree open heavens over my prayers, and today, God of heaven and earth will attend to my case. My prayers today will shake the heavens and move the earth; testimonies, miracles, healing, breakthrough, signs and wonders will follow my prayers. At the end of this prayer session, my life will never be the same again.

PRAYER POINTS

1. O God my Father, thank you for being my God, my Father and my friend.
2. O God my Father, thank you for the privilege to know you and the power of the resurrection of Jesus Christ.
3. O God my Father, thank you for always being there for me and with me.

4. O God my Father, thank you for the great and mighty things that you are doing in my life.
5. O God my Father, thank you for your provision and protection over me and my household.
6. O God my Father, thank you for always answering my prayers.
7. I confess my sins before you today and I ask you to forgive me on the basis of your mercy, in the name of Jesus Christ.
8. Wash me clean today O Lord by the blood of Jesus Christ.
9. I cover myself and my household with the blood of Jesus Christ.
10. My prayers today will not go in vain; my prayers will produce the desired results in the name of Jesus Christ.
11. O God my Father, thank you for being my God, my Father and my friend.
12. O God my Father, thank you for the privilege to know you, and the power of the resurrection of Jesus Christ.
13. O God my Father, thank you for always being there for me and with me.
14. O God my Father, thank you for the great and mighty things that you are doing in my life.
15. O God my Father, thank you for your provision and protection over me and my household.
16. O God my Father, thank you for always answering my prayers.
17. I confess my sins before you today, and I ask you to forgive me on the basis of your mercy, in the name of Jesus Christ.
18. Wash me clean today O Lord by the blood of Jesus Christ.

19. I cover myself and my household with the blood of Jesus Christ.
20. My prayers today will not go in vain; my prayers will produce the desired results, in the name of Jesus Christ.
21. I bind the devil and shut the door to stop his attack against my life, in the name of Jesus Christ.
22. I bind the devil and shut the door to stop his attack against my family, in the name of Jesus Christ.
23. I bind the devil and shut the door to stop his attack against my spouse, in the name of Jesus Christ.
24. I bind the devil and shut the door to stop his attack against my children, in the name of Jesus Christ.
25. I bind the devil and shut the door to stop his attack against my marriage, in the name of Jesus Christ.
26. I bind the devil and shut the door to stop his attack against my business, in the name of Jesus Christ.
27. I bind the devil and shut the door to stop his attack against my job, in the name of Jesus Christ.
28. I bind the devil and shut the door to stop his attack against my finances, in the name of Jesus Christ.
29. I bind the devil and shut the door to stop his attack against my joy, in the name of Jesus Christ.
30. I bind the devil and shut the door to stop his attack against my success, in the name of Jesus Christ.
31. I bind the devil and shut the door to stop his attack against my destiny, in the name of Jesus Christ.
32. I bind the devil and shut the door to stop his attack against my future, in the name of Jesus Christ.
33. I bind the devil and shut the door to stop his attack against my spouse's future, in the name of Jesus Christ.
34. I bind the devil and shut the door to stop his attack against my children's future, in the name of Jesus Christ.

35. I bind the devil and shut the door to stop his attack against my goals and dreams, in the name of Jesus Christ.

36. I bind the devil and shut the door to stop his attack against the plan of God for my life, in the name of Jesus Christ.

37. I bind the devil and shut the door to stop his attack against my health, in the name of Jesus Christ.

38. I bind the devil and shut the door to stop his attack against the works of my hands, in the name of Jesus Christ.

39. I bind the devil and shut the door to stop his attack against the promises of God for me, in the name of Jesus Christ.

40. I bind the devil and shut the door to stop his attack against my quiet enjoyment, in the name of Jesus Christ.

41. I shut the door against the plan of the devil to bring curses upon me, in the name of Jesus Christ.

42. Every plan of the devil to inflict me with sickness, I shut the door against it and I cancel it today, in the name of Jesus Christ.

43. Every plan of the devil to attack me with poverty, I shut the door against it and I cancel it today, in the name of Jesus Christ.

44. Every plan of the devil to attack my marriage, I shut the door against it and I cancel it today, in the name of Jesus Christ.

45. Every plan of the devil to raise opposition against me, I shut the door against it and I cancel it today, in the name of Jesus Christ.

46. Every plan of the devil to raise opposition against me at work, I shut the door against it and I cancel it today, in the name of Jesus Christ.
47. Every plan of the devil to raise opposition against me at home, I shut the door against it and I cancel it today, in the name of Jesus Christ.
48. Today, I shut the door against any form of spiritual attack, in the name of Jesus Christ.
49. Today, I shut the door against any form of sickness or infirmity in my life, in the name of Jesus Christ.
50. Today, I shut the door against the spirit of almost-there in my life, in the name of Jesus Christ.
51. Today, I shut the door against principalities and powers working against me, in the name of Jesus Christ.
52. Today, I shut the door against spiritual wickedness working against me, in the name of Jesus Christ.
53. Today, I shut the door against household wickedness working against me, in the name of Jesus Christ.
54. Today, I shut the door against the power of non-achievement in my life, in the name of Jesus Christ.
55. Today, I shut the door against the spirit of stagnancy in my life, in the name of Jesus Christ.
56. Today, I shut the door against the spirit of failure at the edge of success, in the name of Jesus Christ.
57. Today, I shut the door against the spirit of failure at the edge of breakthrough, in the name of Jesus Christ.
58. Today, I shut the door against the spirit of failure at the edge of miracle, in the name of Jesus Christ.
59. Today, I shut the door against the spirit of empty pocket, in the name of Jesus Christ.
60. Today, I shut the door against every ancestral evil flow, in the name of Jesus Christ.

61. Today, I shut the door against every inherited failure, in the name of Jesus Christ.
62. Today, I shut the door against ancestral curses manifesting in my life, in the name of Jesus Christ.
63. Today, I shut the door against ancestral sickness manifesting in my life, in the name of Jesus Christ.
64. Today, I shut the door against any power assigned to stop my progress, in the name of Jesus Christ.
65. Today, I shut the door against any power assigned to hinder my miracle, in the name of Jesus Christ.
66. Today, I shut the door against any power assigned to cause me pain, in the name of Jesus Christ.
67. Today, I shut the door against any power assigned to frustrate me, in the name of Jesus Christ.
68. Today, I shut the door against any power assigned to delay my blessings, in the name of Jesus Christ.
69. Today, I shut the door against any power assigned to hinder my breakthrough, in the name of Jesus Christ.
70. Today, I shut the door against any power assigned to stop what God is doing in my life, in the name of Jesus Christ.
71. Today, I shut the door against any power assigned to make my life a living hell, in the name of Jesus Christ.
72. Today, I shut the door against any power assigned to trouble me, in the name of Jesus Christ.
73. Today, I shut the door against any power assigned to trouble my marriage, in the name of Jesus Christ.
74. Today, I shut the door against any power assigned to trouble my children, in the name of Jesus Christ.
75. Today, I shut the door against any power assigned to trouble my family, in the name of Jesus Christ.

76. Today, I shut the door against any power assigned to make my life miserable, in the name of Jesus Christ.
77. Today, I shut the door against every evil network working against me, in the name of Jesus Christ.
78. Today, I shut the door against evil network working against my ministry, in the name of Jesus Christ.
79. I shut the door against evil network working against my marriage, in the name of Jesus Christ.
80. I shut the door against every persecution planned against me, in the name of Jesus Christ.
81. I shut the door against any form of bondage in my life, in the name of Jesus Christ.
82. I shut the door against evil activities manifesting in my life, in the name of Jesus Christ.
83. I shut the door against evil activities manifesting in my finances, in the name of Jesus Christ.
84. I shut the door against evil activities manifesting in my business, in the name of Jesus Christ.
85. I shut the door against evil activities manifesting in my children's school, in the name of Jesus Christ.
86. I shut the door against evil activities manifesting in my place of work, in the name of Jesus Christ.
87. I shut the door against evil activities manifesting in my home, in the name of Jesus Christ.
88. I shut the door against evil activities manifesting in my church, in the name of Jesus Christ.
89. I shut the door against evil activities manifesting in my marriage, in the name of Jesus Christ.
90. I shut the door against evil activities manifesting in my neighborhood, in the name of Jesus Christ.
91. I shut the door against the spirit of devourer assigned against me, in the name of Jesus Christ.

92. I shut the door against the spirit of financial embarrassment assigned against me, in the name of Jesus Christ.
93. I shut the door against the spirit of fear tormenting me day and night, in the name of Jesus Christ.
94. I shut the door against the spirit of anger robbing me of my blessings, in the name of Jesus Christ.
95. I shut the door against the spirit of unbelief robbing me of my miracles, in the name of Jesus Christ.
96. I shut the door against the spirit of doubt robbing me of my miracles, in the name of Jesus Christ.
97. I shut the door against any power assigned to scatter what I have gathered, in the name of Jesus Christ.
98. I shut the door against any power assigned to renew my problems, in the name of Jesus Christ.
99. I shut the door against any power assigned to renew my struggles, in the name of Jesus Christ.

I cover my prayers in the blood of Jesus Christ. According to the Word of God, I have asked, I shall receive. I have knocked the door, it shall be opened unto me. I have sought, I shall find, in the name of Jesus Christ. It is written, "… Decree a thing, and it shall be established". As I have spoken in prayer, it shall be so. My prayers shall produce desire results. My prayers shall produce desired miracles. My prayers shall produce desired testimonies, in the name of Jesus Christ. Territorial spirit and power cannot hinder this prayer. Sins and flesh cannot hinder this prayer. It is done. It is sealed by the blood of Jesus Christ. It is delivered to me, in Jesus might name. Amen!

DAY THIRTEEN

O GOD OF ELIJAH, SEND DOWN FIRE

Passages To Read Before You Pray:
2 Kings 1:9-14, 1 Kings 18:22-39, Hebrews 12:29,
Psalms 35, 109, 68

In the book of Job 22:28, the Scripture says when I decree a thing, it shall be established for me. I stand on this Scripture and decree. I have come into the presence of God today to plead my case. I enter through the gate of praise, into the sanctuary of heaven. I cover myself in the precious blood of Jesus Christ. I baptize myself in the fire of the Holy Ghost. I charge this atmosphere with the fire of God, and I take this neighborhood for the Lord. I arrest every principality and power, territorial spirit, and every throne and kingdom that is not of God. I cast you down and I command you never to lift yourself up against me, because I have the life of God in me.

In the name of Jesus Christ, I confess my sins today, and I ask you O Lord to forgive me on the basis of your mercy. With all my heart, I forgive those who have sinned against me; from the past through this moment. I release them from any form of guilt and shame, in the name of Jesus Christ. I hereby plead the blood of Jesus over any sins committed by my parents and ancestors. I cancel through the Blood of Jesus Christ, any satanic covenants, exchanges, vows or transactions, made over my life, body, soul, spirit, and circumstances, in the name of Jesus Christ. I cancel every legal right that the devil may have against me, by the blood of Jesus Christ. The accuser of the brethren will have nothing against me, as I come to the presence of God in prayer.

The devil cannot hinder or delay my prayer, because I know who I am. I am a child of the Kingdom. I am a king and priest of the Lord, redeemed from the hand of the devil by the blood of Jesus Christ. I walk in power. I walk in miracle. Proverbs 18:21 says, death and life are in the power of my tongue; I command the power in my tongue to manifest now. I command my tongue to become fire, to consume all the powers of darkness in the air, the land, the sea, and beneath the earth. I hereby raise Holy Ghost standard against the prince of the power of the air and all the hosts of darkness in the air. I raise Holy Ghost standard against the queen of the coasts and all the hosts of darkness on the land. I raise Holy Ghost standard against the marine kingdom and all the hosts of darkness in the sea. I raise Holy Ghost standard against the kingdom of hell and all the hosts of darkness beneath the earth. I shoot down all the networks of demons gathering to resist my prayers. I rebuke and bind all the controlling forces of darkness standing against my prayers.

I declare that all satanic thrones, altars, dominions, principalities, powers, rulers of darkness, queens of the coast, queens of heavens, household wickedness, spiritual hosts of wickedness and all satanic works, have no power or authority over my life. I declare that satanic harassment and intimidation have no effect on me.

Today, I receive divine strength to pray; I will not pray in vain. I will not pray amiss. My prayers will bring the desired results. I command the fountain of prayer to open now, and to flow into my life, I command the warring angels of God to descend and fight on my behalf. Every minute and every hour that I spend in prayer, will bring solution. Every prayer point will attract divine attention and divine intervention. I decree open heavens over my prayers, and today, God of heaven and earth will attend to my case. My prayers today will shake the heavens and move the earth. Testimonies, miracles, healings, breakthroughs, and signs and wonders, will follow my prayers. At the end of this prayer session, my life will never be the same again.

PRAYER POINTS

1. O God my Father, thank you for being my God, my Father and my friend.
2. O God my Father, thank you for the privilege to know you and the power of the resurrection of Jesus Christ.
3. O God my Father, thank you for always being there for me and with me.
4. O God my Father, thank you for the great and mighty things that you are doing in my life.
5. O God my Father, thank you for your provision and protection over me and my household.
6. O God my Father, thank you for always answering my prayers.
7. I confess my sins before you today and I ask you to forgive me on the basis of your mercy, in the name of Jesus Christ.
8. Wash me clean today O Lord by the blood of Jesus Christ.
9. I cover myself and my household with the blood of Jesus Christ.
10. My prayers today will not go in vain; my prayers will produce the desired results in the name of Jesus Christ.
11. As Elijah called the fire of God to fall and consume the sacrifice on Mount Carmel, I call upon the fire of God

today to consume every work of the devil manifesting as poverty in my life, in the name of Jesus Christ.

12. As Elijah called the fire of God to fall and consume the sacrifice on Mount Carmel, I call upon the fire of God today to consume every work of the devil manifesting as failure in my life, in the name of Jesus Christ.

13. As Elijah called the fire of God to fall and consume the sacrifice on Mount Carmel, I call upon the fire of God today to consume every work of the devil manifesting as sickness in my body, in the name of Jesus Christ.

14. As Elijah called the fire of God to fall and consume the sacrifice on Mount Carmel, I call upon the fire of God today to consume every work of the devil manifesting as backwardness in my life, in the name of Jesus Christ.

15. As Elijah called the fire of God to fall and consume the sacrifice on Mount Carmel, I call upon the fire of God today to consume every work of the devil manifesting as stagnation in my life, in the name of Jesus Christ.

16. As Elijah called the fire of God to fall and consume the sacrifice on Mount Carmel, I call upon the fire of God today to consume every work of the devil manifesting as procrastination in my life, in the name of Jesus Christ.

17. As Elijah called the fire of God to fall and consume the sacrifice on Mount Carmel, I call upon the fire of God today to consume every work of the devil manifesting as curses upon my life, in the name of Jesus Christ.

18. As Elijah called the fire of God to fall and consume the sacrifice on Mount Carmel, I call upon the fire of God today to consume every work of the devil manifesting as bondages in my life, in the name of Jesus Christ.

19. As Elijah called the fire of God to fall and consume the sacrifice on Mount Carmel, I call upon the fire of God

today to consume every work of the devil manifesting as burdens upon my life, in the name of Jesus Christ.

20. As Elijah called the fire of God to fall and consume the sacrifice on Mount Carmel, I call upon the fire of God today to consume every work of the devil manifesting as delay in my life, in the name of Jesus Christ.

21. As Elijah called the fire of God to fall and consume the sacrifice on Mount Carmel, I call upon the fire of God today to consume every work of the devil manifesting as infirmities in my life, in the name of Jesus Christ.

22. As Elijah called the fire of God to fall and consume the sacrifice on Mount Carmel, I call upon the fire of God today to consume every work of the devil manifesting as problems in my life, in the name of Jesus Christ.

23. As Elijah called the fire of God to fall and consume the sacrifice on Mount Carmel, I call upon the fire of God today to consume every work of the devil manifesting as frustration in my life, in the name of Jesus Christ.

24. As Elijah called the fire of God to fall and consume the sacrifice on Mount Carmel, I call upon the fire of God today to consume every work of the devil manifesting as depression in my life, in the name of Jesus Christ.

25. As Elijah called the fire of God to fall and consume the sacrifice on Mount Carmel, I call upon the fire of God today to consume every work of the devil manifesting as barrenness in my life, in the name of Jesus Christ.

26. As Elijah called the fire of God to fall and consume the sacrifice on Mount Carmel, I call upon the fire of God today to consume every work of the devil manifesting as loneliness in my life, in the name of Jesus Christ.

27. As Elijah called the fire of God to fall and consume the sacrifice on Mount Carmel, I call upon the fire of God

today to consume every work of the devil manifesting as fear in my life, in the name of Jesus Christ.

28. As Elijah called the fire of God to fall and consume the sacrifice on Mount Carmel, I call upon the fire of God today to consume every work of the devil manifesting as rejection in my life, in the name of Jesus Christ.

29. As Elijah called the fire of God to fall and consume the sacrifice on Mount Carmel, I call upon the fire of God today to consume every work of the devil manifesting as hatred in my life, in the name of Jesus Christ.

30. As Elijah called the fire of God to fall and consume the sacrifice on Mount Carmel, I call upon the fire of God today to consume every work of the devil manifesting as evil mark in my life, in the name of Jesus Christ.

31. As Elijah called the fire of God to fall and consume the sacrifice on Mount Carmel, I call upon the fire of God today to consume every work of the devil manifesting as evil garment upon me, in the name of Jesus Christ.

I cover my prayers in the blood of Jesus Christ. According to the Word of God, I have asked; I shall receive. I have knocked the door; it shall be opened unto me. I have sought; I shall find, in the name of Jesus Christ. It is written, "… Decree a thing, and it shall be established". As I have spoken in prayer, it shall be so. My prayers shall produce desired results. My prayers shall produce desired miracles. My prayers shall produce desired testimonies, in the name of Jesus Christ. Territorial spirit and power cannot hinder this prayer. Sins and flesh cannot hinder this prayer. It is done. It is sealed by the blood of Jesus Christ. It is delivered to me, in Jesus mighty name. Amen!

DAY FOURTEEN

PRAYER TO FIGHT WITHOUT FEAR

Passages To Read Before You Pray:

Isaiah 27:10, Jeremiah 1:8, 19, Isaiah 45:2-3,
Psalms 27, 69, 55, 35, 68

In the book of Job 22:28, the Scripture says when I decree a thing, it shall be established for me. I stand on this Scripture and decree. I have come into the presence of God today to plead my case. I enter through the gate of praise into the sanctuary of heaven. I cover myself in the precious blood of Jesus Christ. I baptize myself in the fire of the Holy Ghost. I charge this atmosphere with the fire of God, and I take this neighborhood for the Lord. I arrest every principality and power, territorial spirit, and every throne and kingdom that is not of God. I cast you down and I command you never to lift yourself up against me, because I have the life of God in me.

In the name of Jesus Christ, I confess my sins today, and I ask you O Lord to forgive me on the basis of your mercy. With all my heart, I forgive those who have sinned against me from the past through this moment. I release them from any form of guilt and shame, in the name of Jesus Christ. I hereby plead the blood of Jesus over any sins committed by my parents and ancestors. I cancel through the Blood of Jesus Christ, any satanic covenants, exchanges, vows or transactions made over my life, body, soul, spirit, and circumstances, in the name of Jesus Christ. I cancel every legal right that the devil may have against me, by the blood of Jesus Christ. The accuser of the brethren will have nothing against me as I come to the presence of God in prayer.

The devil cannot hinder or delay my prayer, because I know who I am. I am a child of the Kingdom; I am a king and priest of the Lord, redeemed from the hand of the devil by the blood of Jesus Christ. I declare that all satanic thrones, altars, dominions, principalities, powers, rulers of darkness, queen of the coast, queen of heavens, household wickedness, spiritual hosts of wickedness and all satanic works, have no power or authority over my life. I declare that satanic harassment and intimidation have no effect on me.

Today I receive divine strength to pray; I will not pray in vain. I will not pray amiss. My prayers will bring the desired results. I command the fountain of prayer to open now, and flow into my life, I command the warring angels of God to descend and fight on my behalf. Every minute and every hour that I spend in prayer will bring solution. Every prayer point will attract divine attention and divine intervention. I decree open heavens over my prayers, and today, God of heaven and earth will attend to my case. My prayers today will shake the heavens and move the earth; testimonies, miracles, healing, breakthrough, signs and wonders will follow my prayers. At the end of this prayer session, my life will never be the same again.

PRAYER POINTS

1. O God my Father, thank you for being my God, my Father and my friend.
2. O God my Father, thank you for the privilege to know you and the power of the resurrection of Jesus Christ.
3. O God my Father, thank you for always being there for me and with me.

4. O God my Father, thank you for the great and mighty things that you are doing in my life.
5. O God my Father, thank you for your provision and protection over me and my household.
6. O God my Father, thank you for always answering my prayers.
7. I confess my sins before you today and I ask you to forgive me on the basis of your mercy, in the name of Jesus Christ.
8. Wash me clean today O Lord by the blood of Jesus Christ.
9. I cover myself and my household with the blood of Jesus Christ.
10. My prayers today will not go in vain; my prayers will produce the desired results in the name of Jesus Christ.
11. O God my Father, let the remaining months of this year be better for me than the last eight months, in the name of Jesus Christ.
12. O God my Father, let your grace rescue me from hardship and struggle; I have had enough.
13. O God my Father, let your power rescue me from the pit of hopelessness. Arise today, and set me free, in the name of Jesus Christ.
14. Every evil covering that will not let my helpers see me, be destroyed now by fire, in the name of Jesus Christ.
15. Satanic embargoes holding my life back, be destroyed now by fire, in the name of Jesus Christ.
16. Today, I receive the anointing of ease to breakthrough before the end of this year, in the name of Jesus Christ.
17. Today, I receive the anointing of ease to have great achievements before the end of this year, in the name of Jesus Christ.

18. Today, I receive the anointing and power to overcome obstacles in my way, in the name of Jesus Christ.
19. O God my Father, arise and make my dream a reality before the end of this year, in the name of Jesus Christ.
20. O God my Father, for how long would I wait and expect? Arise today and answer my prayers, in the name of Jesus Christ.
21. O God my Father, for how long would I wait and expect? Arise today and connect me to the people that will help me, in the name of Jesus Christ.
22. O God my Father, it is not your plan for me to suffer but to succeed in life, arise today O Lord, and fulfill your plan in my life, in the name of Jesus Christ.
23. O God my Father, for how long would I wait and expect? Arise today and deliver me from this miserable situation, in the name of Jesus Christ.
24. O God my Father, for how long would you allow the enemy to terrorize and torment me? Arise today and fight for me, in the name of Jesus Christ.
25. O God my Father, I am tired of my situation, arise today and change my story for the better, in the name of Jesus Christ.
26. I receive wisdom to neutralize the plans, techniques and strategies of the enemy working against me, in the name of Jesus Christ.
27. I release the fire of God to destroy all the ammunition of the enemy prepared against me, in the name of Jesus Christ.
28. I release the fire of God to destroy the stronghold of the enemy working against me, in the name of Jesus Christ.

29. O God my Father, release the warring angels to make a way for me, where there seems to be no way this month, in the name of Jesus Christ.

30. O God my Father, release the warring angels to go before me and destroy obstacles in my way this month, in the name of Jesus Christ.

31. O God my Father, release the warring angels to go before me and destroy every agent of darkness that lays in ambush to attack me, in the name of Jesus Christ.

32. I receive wisdom and power to overcome the power of the enemy sent to create problems for me, in the name of Jesus Christ.

33. I receive wisdom and power to overcome every situation designed to create problems for me, in the name of Jesus Christ.

34. I receive wisdom and power to overcome every agent of darkness sent to create problems for me, in the name of Jesus Christ.

35. O God my Father, surround me with strong and fearless prayer warriors that will pray with me to overcome my long-time problems, in the name of Jesus Christ.

36. O God my Father, surround me with strong and fearless prayer warriors that will pray with me to conquer the battle that I have been fighting all my life, in the name of Jesus Christ.

37. O God my Father, surround me with strong and fearless prayer warriors that will pray with me until I have my breakthroughs, in the name of Jesus Christ.

38. O God my Father, surround me with strong and fearless prayer warriors that will pray with me until I am delivered from this stubborn situation, in the name of Jesus Christ.

39. O God my Father, arise today and surround me with your fire, so that the enemy will not be able to touch me, in the name of Jesus Christ.
40. Today, I receive courage to move forward without fear no matter the activities of the enemy, in the name of Jesus Christ.
41. O God my Father, I am tired of fighting. Arise today and fight for me, in the name of Jesus Christ.
42. O God my Father, let your fire pursue my enemies to the point of no return, that they will never lift their heads against me again, in the name of Jesus Christ.
43. O God my Father, release your fire today and destroy the plan of the enemy concerning my life, in the name of Jesus Christ.
44. O God my Father, arise today and trouble those that trouble me, in the name of Jesus Christ.
45. O God my Father, arise today and fight against those that fight against me, in the name of Jesus Christ.
46. O God my Father, arise and scatter every satanic network working against me by your fire, in the name of Jesus Christ.
47. O God arise and let my household wickedness be scattered, in the name of Jesus Christ.
48. O God arise and let all my enemies be scattered, in the name of Jesus Christ.
49. O God my Father, arise and let the everlasting door of failure built against me be destroyed by fire, in the name of Jesus Christ.
50. O God my Father, arise and let the everlasting door of infirmity built against me be destroyed by fire, in the name of Jesus Christ.

I cover my prayers in the blood of Jesus Christ. According to the Word of God, I have asked, I shall receive. I have knocked the door, it shall be opened unto me. I have sought, I shall find, in the name of Jesus Christ. It is written, "... Decree a thing, and it shall be established". As I have spoken in prayer, it shall be so. My prayers shall produce desire results. My prayers shall produce desired miracles. My prayers shall produce desired testimonies, in the name of Jesus Christ. Territorial spirit and power cannot hinder this prayer. Sins and flesh cannot hinder this prayer. It is done. It is sealed by the blood of Jesus Christ. It is delivered to me, in Jesus might name. Amen!

I Must Win This Battle

I Must Win This Battle offers a hands-on training self-deliverance process and prayers. It covers over 2000 prayer points focusing on how to remove unpleasant and unwanted situations of life. Battle of life is a must win for every child of God and this book shows how to, in a very simple and effective way. It is a must have for every household.

Let There Be A Change

"Let There Be A Change" is a must have Personal Deliverance prayer book that will transform your life and bring restoration into every area of your life. What is Deliverance? Deliverance means to loose the bounds of wickedness. A lot of people are under the bondage of wickedness. If you look at the lives of many people, you will discover a wide array of wicked occurrences. If your life is surrounded by wicked mysterious happenings, you need to seek deliverance as soon as possible. Deliverance centers on the destruction of the yoke of the enemy. A yoke is anything that hinders or sets you back. Whatever sets you back from moving forward in your life is a yoke. God's will is that you move forward and attain divine goals set for your life. When the contrary happens, there is a bondage hanging above your life. Deliverance is to break curses and evil covenants. The ancestors of many people were cursed and the curses have flown down the family line. For example, if a person struggles without any tangible achievement in life, there is a problem somewhere.

Earth Moving Prayers

"I have seen the affliction of my people, and have heard their cry by reason of their enemies and tormentors, for I know their sorrows; and I have come down to deliver them out of the hand of the wicked and unrepentant enemies. And I will surely bring to pass my plans and counsels concerning them." This is the Word of the Lord that gave birth to this Anointed Prayer Book, "EARTH-MOVING PRAYERS". Earth-Moving Prayers is a highly anointed deliverance prayer book that will transform your life, and set you free from any form of bondage or captivity you may find yourself. Over 600 pages of mountain moving and yoke destroying prayer points. Over 5300 problems solving and solution finding prayer points prepared by the Holy Ghost to set you free. If you are ready to take your life back from that terrible situation, this book is for you, a must have for every household.

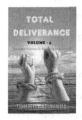

Total Deliverance – Volume 1

"Why would you pay for a debt that you did not owe? Why would you have to be what the enemies want your life to be? The plan of God for you is to live freely and prosper as He has promised in the Scriptures. You do not have to pay for the sins of your parents or ancestors; you don't have to go through what they went through, your life is different and your case is different. If you can just believe, the Bible says, "You will see the glory of God." – John 11:40.

This book is loaded with prayers that will transform your life, deliver you from ancestral curses, generational and foundational curses, self-inflicted curses, break yokes and destroy bondages no matter how long it's been there."

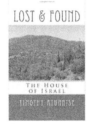

Lost & Found: The House of Israel

Lost & Found "The House of Israel" offers detailed information about the past, present and future of the House of Israel. Jacob released special blessings upon two of his children, he gave Joseph the Birthright and Judah the Kingdom. God made covenant with David that he will always have a son on his throne and his throne will be everlasting. In this book, you will discover where the throne of David is currently and how it got there. It is a must for every Bible student.

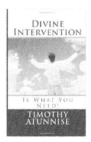

Divine Intervention

Deliverance centers on the destruction of the yoke of the enemy. A yoke is anything that hinders or sets you back. Whatever sets you back from moving forward in your life is a yoke.

God's will is that you move forward and attain divine goals set for your life. When the contrary happens, there is a bondage hanging above your life.

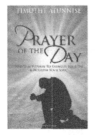

Prayer of The Day – Volume 1

How wonderful would it be to start your day with joy and end it with great success? The Spirit of the Lord led me to write Prayer of the Day, a wonderful, daily spiritual vitamin. He promised that this book would touch and change many lives and situations for the better as people began to commit every day to the hands of God, for He knows the beginning and ending. Prayer is communion with God. Through prayer we actually experience relationship with God. The quality of our prayer life determines the quality of our relationship with God. I promise you, in the name of the Lord, that you will experience the power of God, great deliverance and a move of the Holy Spirit in your life as you join millions of people across the globe in prayer every morning before you start your day.

Prayer of The Day – Volume 2

How wonderful would it be to start your day with joy and end it with great success? The Spirit of the Lord led me to write Prayer of the Day, a wonderful, daily spiritual vitamin. He promised that this book would touch and change many lives and situations for

148

the better as people began to commit every day to the hands of God, for He knows the beginning and ending. Prayer is communion with God. Through prayer we actually experience relationship with God. The quality of our prayer life determines the quality of our relationship with God. I promise you, in the name of the Lord, that you will experience the power of God, great deliverance and a move of the Holy Spirit in your life as you join millions of people across the globe in prayer every morning before you start your day.

Overcoming Self

Sunday School manual

The King Is Coming

The King Is Coming teaches the End-Times messages and prophecies. It is very accurate and easy to understand. It shows the application of the Word of God to current affairs, and establishing the truth of what is happening in world today in the Scripture. It is written to prepare the Saints for that Glorious Hope and for the End-Times assignments (End-Times Revival).

The Fruit of The Spirit

Fruit of the Spirit is mentioned in several areas of the Bible. However, the most applicable passage is Galatians 5:22-23 where Paul actually lists out the fruits. Paul used this list to show the contrast between a Godly character and one that is focused on fleshly concerns. These are not just individual "fruits" (attributes) from which to pick and choose. Rather, the fruit of the Spirit is one ninefold "fruit" that characterizes all who truly walk in the Holy Spirit. In order to understand the fruit of the Spirit, we must first understand who the Spirit is, what He does and how He helps us live our lives pleasing to God. The questions are: What are the Fruits of the Spirit? How can you develop them? What does that mean for you? What fruits of the Spirit do you have?

The Parables of Jesus Christ

A parable is a story in which a real and earthly thing is used to parallel or illustrate a spiritual or heavenly thing. Such a story acts as a "riddle" that both veils and reveals all at once -- veiling the spiritual behind words that reveal the earthly and which can be penetrated to reach the spiritual by those "who have ears to hear." Jesus tells us that He spoke in parables precisely to veil and reveal, to speak, in a sense, "secretly" while not in secret at all.

The Miracles of Jesus Christ

Understanding the story of the healing and miracles of Jesus Christ. Christ came into the world, not only as God's personal representative on earth, but as God manifest in flesh. He was Himself a miracle in human form, and His miraculous works are bound up inseparably with His life. "The blind receive their sight and the lame walk; the lepers are cleansed and the deaf hear; the dead are raised up and the poor have the gospel preached to them". His miracles provided proof of who He was.

Bible Study: The Book of Exodus

This Bible study is designed as an expository study of the Book of Exodus, taking the student through large portions of this Old Testament book with cross references to other portions of Scripture. The purpose is to assist the student in gaining a greater comprehension of the biblical teaching contained in the Book of Exodus with an emphasis on practical application. This study presents introductory information about the Book of Exodus followed by twenty-two lessons devoted to an in-depth study of the biblical text. The student will begin by exploring a portion of Exodus with the help of a series of exploratory questions. There will then follow an in-depth study of the passage, guided by an expositional commentary on the text. The student should prepare for his study by asking the Holy Spirit to enlighten his mind and open his heart to receive not only the teaching of Scripture but Christ Himself as He is presented in the Scriptures.

Essential Prayers:
(Prayers That Bring Total Victory)

Essential Prayers is an anointed prayer book that touches every aspect of life. It offers ways to make prayers more personal and powerful, and how to establish a practice of prayer that works.
Essential Prayers is for every Christian home, it will surely transform your prayer life and reshape your entire outlook of life.

Essential Prayers addresses your personal situations, it provides prayers for marriage restoration, total victory, financial release, deliverance from addiction, prayer against problems started in childhood, foundational problems, prayer for singles, prayer against ancestral debt-collectors, prayer for signs and wonders, and many more.

We are given the authority and power to take over, not to be run over. If you fail to take over, you'll be run over. Essential Prayers offers step-by-step prayer guidelines to take over and possess your possessions.

PRAYER CDs by TIMOTHY ATUNNISE

1. Pray Before You Start Your Day
2. Pray Before You Go To Bed
3. Overcoming Impossibilities
4. Prayer To Overcome Poverty
5. Prayer To Break Evil Cycles
6. Prayer To Stop Demonic Activities
7. Prayer For Business Prosperity
8. Secret of Finding God's Rest
9. Spiritual House Cleansing
10. Take Your Life Back By Force
11. Prayer To Overcome Limitations
12. Prayer To Cancel Untimely Death
13. Prayer To Break Curses of Poverty & Empty Pocket
14. Prayer For Victory Over Bad Dreams
15. Prayer For Uncommon Favor
16. Prayer For Supernatural Breakthroughs
17. Prayer To Break Ungodly Soul-Ties
18. Prayer To Overcome Financial Setbacks
19. Prayer To Destroy The Works of The Devil
20. Prayer To Overturn Stubborn Situations
21. Prayer To Close Evil Chapters
22. Prayer For Instant Miracles
23. Shaping Your Children's Future
24. Prayer For Restoration
25. I Must Win This Battle
26. The Secret of Knowing God

DELIVERANCE PRAYER CDs by TIMOTHY ATUNNISE

1. Prayer For Self-Deliverance
2. Healing The Wounded Heart
3. Prevention & Deliverance From Cancer
4. Deliverance From Evil Covenant
5. Deliverance From The Devourer
6. Deliverance & Healing Prayer
7. Identify Your Spiritual Territory (Parts 1 & 2)
8. Exercise Spiritual Authority
9. Casting Out Spirits   (Parts 1 & 2)
10. Curses & How To Deal With Them   (Parts 1 & 2)
11. How Demons Enter & Oppress People (Parts 1 & 2)
12. Deliverance From Jezebel's Spirit
13. Defeating The Strongman
14. Deliverance From The Terrible
15. Deliverance From Curses of Last-Minute Failure
16. Deliverance From Curses of Rejection

WORSHIP CDs

1. Christocentric – Worship Songs
2. I Am That I Am
3. Yahweh Reigns

Note

Note